Junior
Encyclopedia

First published in 2006 by Bardfield Press
Copyright © Miles Kelly Publishing Ltd 2006

Bardfield Press is an imprint of
Miles Kelly Publishing Ltd
Bardfield Centre, Great Bardfield, Essex, CM7 4SL

2 4 6 8 10 9 7 5 3 1

Editorial Director Belinda Gallagher

Art Director Jo Brewer

Editor Amanda Askew

Assistant Editor Lucy Dowling

Designers Jo Brewer, Tom Slemmings

Production Elizabeth Brunwin

Reprographics Anthony Cambray, Mike Coupe, Stephan Davis,
Liberty Newton, Ian Paulyn

Indexer Jane Parker

ISBN 10: 1-84236-776-5
ISBN 13: 978-1-84236-776-6

Printed in China

British Library Cataloguing-in-Publication Data
A catalogue record for this book is available from the British Library

www.mileskelly.net
info@mileskelly.net

All artworks are from MKP Archives

Junior
Encyclopedia

BARDFIELD
PRESS

Contents

Space

Space is everywhere 14
Our life-giving star 16
The planet family 18
Earth in space 20
Earth – our home 22
Earth's neighbours 24
Tiny planets 26
Massive planets 28
Far, far away 30
Birth of a star 32
So many galaxies 34
Exploring the sky 36
Launching into space 38
Life in space 40
At home in space 42
Exploring with robots 44
Spies in space 46
Off to the Moon 48

Planet Earth

Forming the Earth 52
Inside the Earth 54
Spinning around 56
Rocks can change 58
Violent volcanoes 60
Making mountains 62
Shaking and quaking 64
Lakes and rivers 66
Under the surface 68
Lands of sand 70

Contents

Forests of the world 72
Water, water everywhere 74
Under the ocean 76
Rock pool life 78
Tropical life 80

Weather

Layers of air 84
What is weather? 86
Guessing the weather 88
All the seasons 90
Tropical seasons 92
Scorching Sun 94
Clouds and rain 96
Windy weather 98
Thunder and lightning 100
In a spin! 102
Light shows 104

Science

Our world of science 108
Machines are everywhere 110
Hot science 112
Light at work 114
What a noise! 116
Magnet power 118
What is electricity? 120
Invisible waves 122
Computer science 124
Laser power 126
Amazing web 128
What is it made of? 130
Mini science 132
Science and nature 134
Healthy science 136

Contents

Dinosaurs

The dinosaur world 140
When were they around? 142
Life before dinosaurs 144
The dinosaurs arrive 146
Changing dinosaurs 148
Gentle giants 150
Huge hunters 152
See, hear, smell 154

Slow or speedy? 156
Eggs and nests 158
Baby dinosaurs 160
Dinosaurs in battle 162
Where did they go? 164
What they left behind 166
Finding fossils 168

Oceans

Sea mammals 172
Cold-blooded creatures 174
Deep-sea creatures 176
Super swimmers 178
Awesome jaws 180
Fast flippers 182
Great travellers 184
Air aces 186
All kinds of penguin 188

Contents

Mammals

What are mammals? 192
Mammal families 194
Baby mammals 196
Tallest and smallest 198
Top racers 200
High fliers 202
Champion diggers 204
River mammals 206
Snow mammals 208
Fins and flippers 210
In the rainforest 212
Desert life 214

Plant eaters 216
Hungry hunters 218

Birds

Birds everywhere 222
The bird world 224
Biggest and smallest 226
Starting life 228
Family life 230
Bird homes 232
Fast fliers 234
Swimmers and divers 236
Night birds 238
Feeding time 240
Fierce hunters 242
Rainforest birds 244
Snow birds 246
River life 248

Contents

Bugs

Creepy-crawlies 252
Insects everywhere! 254
Is it an insect? 256
Insect homes 258
Flapping around 260
Hop, skip and jump 262
Speedy bugs 264
Swimmers and skaters 266
Burrowing bugs 268
Bites and stings 270
Hide and seek 272
Dinner time 274

What is a spider? 276
The spider world 278
A sting in the tail 280

Ancient Egypt

Life on the Nile 284
Powerful pharaohs 286
Gods and goddesses 288
The great pyramids 290
Temples and tombs 292
Mummification 294
War and weapons 296
Buying and selling 298
Farming the land 300
The working life 302
Life at home 304
Dressing up 306
Travelling by boat 308

Contents

Painting words **310**
Egyptian know-how **312**

Ancient Rome

Rome and its empire **316**
Building Rome **318**
Rulers of Rome **320**
Gods and goddesses **322**
The people of Rome **324**
Family life **326**
Eating and drinking **328**
A trip to the baths **330**
Roman style **332**
Learning new skills **334**
Work and play **336**
The mighty Colosseum **338**
In the army **340**
Roman roads **342**

Knights & Castles

Life in the Middle Ages **346**
The first castles **348**
Building castles **350**
Inside the castle **352**
Castle life **354**
People and power **356**
Knight school **358**
Jousting tournaments **360**
Dress for battle **362**
Brave knights **364**
Famous battles **366**
Fighting back **368**
The crusades **370**
Castle siege **372**

Index **374**

How to use this book

This fantastic book is bursting with information, colour pictures, activities and quizzes. Use these pages to help you find your way around all the fun-packed things to do and read!

Each new topic has an introductory paragraph packed with information

Each image is explained with a caption

Swimmers and divers

Penguins are the best swimmers and divers in the bird world. They live in and around the Antarctic, an icy place at the very south of the world. They spend most of their lives in water, using their wings as strong flippers to help them swim.

▶ The gannet dives into the water, seizes it prey and surfaces a few seconds later.

▼ Emperor penguins can dive for more than 18 minutes.

224

Test your memory with Quiz time! Or you can have fun doing different activities

This heading tells you which section you are in

Birds

Learn more about the main picture with these close-up images

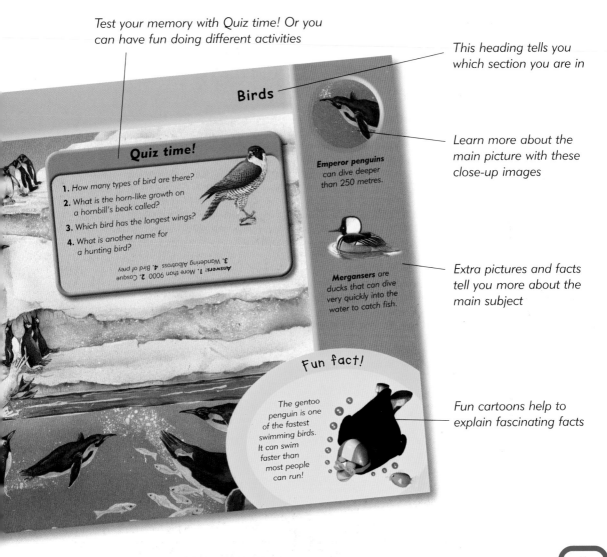

Quiz time!

1. How many types of bird are there?
2. What is the horn-like growth on a hornbill's beak called?
3. Which bird has the longest wings?
4. What is another name for a hunting bird?

Answers: 1. More than 9000 2. Casque 3. Wandering Albatross 4. Bird of prey

Emperor penguins can dive deeper than 250 metres.

Mergansers are ducks that can dive very quickly into the water to catch fish.

Extra pictures and facts tell you more about the main subject

Fun fact!

The gentoo penguin is one of the fastest swimming birds. It can swim faster than most people can run!

Fun cartoons help to explain fascinating facts

Space

Space is all around the Earth, high above the atmosphere. Although space is mostly empty, there are amazing things within it. Read about the Solar System and its family of planets, discover how stars form and die, and take a closer look at how a space station is built.

Space is everywhere

Space is all around the Earth, high above the air. Here on the Earth's surface we are surrounded by air. If you go upwards, up a mountain or in an aircraft, air grows thinner until there is none at all. This is where space begins.

Space shuttle

Astronaut

▶ In space, astronauts wear spacesuits to go outside the space shuttle as it circles the Earth.

Space

Earth

The Earth's atmosphere is a mixture of gases that humans can breathe.

The surface of the Earth is made up of land and sea.

Astronauts are people who travel in space.

Create your own space city

You will need:
cardboard box • silver foil • scissors • glue • empty containers –
plastic bottles, cardboard tubes, cans, yoghurt pots and lids

1. Use the lid of the box as your base and cover it with foil. Cover all the empty containers with foil, too.

2. Cut plastic bottles to make domes. Use tubes and cans to make tunnels and passages, and lids to make satellite dishes.

3. Stick everything to the base and play with your own space city!

15

Our life-giving star

The Sun is our nearest star. It does not look like other stars because it is much closer to us. Most stars are so far away, they look like points of light in the sky. The Sun is not solid like the Earth, but is a giant ball of super-hot gases. These gases are very hot and glow like bonfire flames.

▶ The Sun's hot, glowing gas is always on the move, bubbling up to the surface and sinking back down again.

Prominence (huge loop of gas thrown out into space)

Sunspot

Solar flare

▶ Every so often, the Sun, Moon and Earth line up in space so that the Moon is directly between the Earth and Sun. This stops sunlight from reaching a small area on Earth. The area grows dark and cold, as if night has come early. This is called an eclipse.

Sun

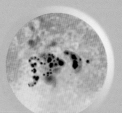

Solar flares are explosions of energy that shoot out from the Sun.

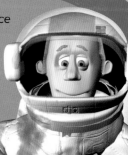

Sunspots are large, cool spots on the surface of the Sun.

Shadow of the eclipse

Moon

Earth

Fun fact!

The surface of the Sun is nearly 60 times hotter than boiling water. It is so hot, it would melt a spacecraft that flew near it.

The planet family

The Sun is surrounded by a family of circling planets called the Solar System. This family is held together by an invisible force called gravity, which pulls things towards each other. It is the same force that pulls us to the ground and stops us floating away. The Sun's gravity pulls on the planets and keeps them travelling around it.

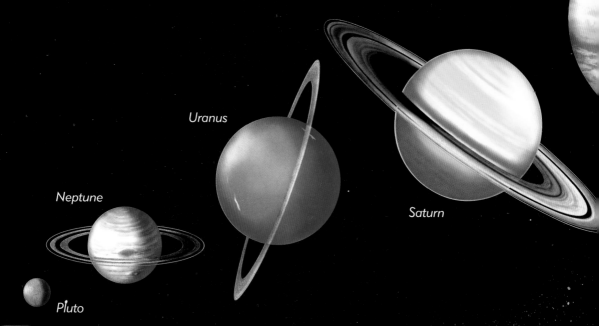

Uranus

Neptune

Saturn

Pluto

Mercury

Moon

Jupiter

Sun

Venus

Earth

Mars

Some planets have rings made up of ice, dust and rocks.

From space, we can see the swirling atmospheres of the planets.

Fun fact!

If the Sun was the size of a large beach ball, the Earth would be as small as a pea, and the Moon would look like a pinhead.

NASA

▲ The nine planets are all different. Mercury, nearest to the Sun, is small and hot. Then Venus, Earth and Mars are rocky and cooler. Beyond them Jupiter, Saturn, Uranus and Neptune are large and cold, while Pluto is tiny and icy.

Earth in space

The Earth moves through space at nearly 3000 metres a second. It weighs 6000 million, million, million tonnes. Up to two-thirds of the Earth's rocky surface is covered by water, making the seas and oceans. Surrounding the Earth is a layer of gases called the atmosphere. This layer stretches 700 kilometres from the Earth's surface.

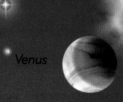

Venus

Sun

Mercury

▲ The Earth is the fifth largest planet in the Solar System. As it spins in space, the Earth bulges in the middle, like a pumpkin.

Space

Moon

Earth

Galaxies are giant groups of millions or even trillions of stars.

A cloud of dust and gas in space is called a nebula.

A star is a ball of very hot gas.

Quiz time!

1. What is the Earth made up of?
2. What is the force called that pulls us to the ground?
3. Who travels in space?
4. What is a star?

Answers: 1. Land and sea **2.** Gravity **3.** Astronaut **4.** Ball of hot gas

21

Earth – our home

The planet we live on is called the Earth. It is a round ball of rock. On the outside where we live, the rock is hard and solid. But deep below our feet, inside the Earth, the rock is hot enough to melt. Sometimes this hot rock showers out of an erupting volcano.

▶ *The Earth is made up of masses of land and water. Surrounding the Earth is the atmosphere, a blanket of gases.*

Fun fact!

The Moon has no air or water. When astronauts went to the Moon they had to take air with them in their spacecraft and spacesuits.

▶ The Moon is very close to the
Earth. It travels around the
Earth, taking one month
to complete its journey.

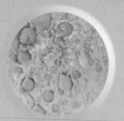

Craters are scars
left by rocks that
have hit the
Moon's surface.

When the Moon
cannot be seen at
all, it is called a
New Moon.

The crust is the
thin surface layer
that we live on.

▼ Over one month, the Moon changes from a thin crescent shape
to a round shape. This is because the Sun lights up one side of the
Moon. The other side is dark. As the Moon circles the Earth, we see
different parts of the lit side.

Crescent Moon   First quarter Moon   Gibbous Moon   Full Moon

Earth's neighbours

Venus and Mars are the nearest planets to the Earth. Venus is closer to the Sun than the Earth while Mars is farther away. Each takes a different amount of time to circle the Sun. This is called a year. A year on Venus is 225 days, on Earth 365 days, and on Mars 687 days.

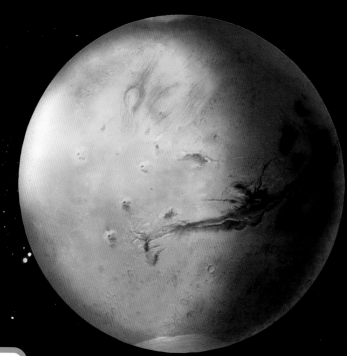

Mars

◄ *Mars is very dry, like a desert, and covered in red dust. Winds on Mars whip up huge dust storms that can cover the whole planet.*

Venus has poisonous clouds with drops of acid that would burn your skin.

Venus

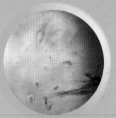

Olympus Mons is the biggest volcano on Mars.

Valles Marineris is an enormous valley that cuts across Mars.

The clouds on Venus race all around the planet in just four days.

Planet spotting

See if you can spot Venus in the night sky. It is often the first bright star to appear in the evening, just above where the Sun has set. Sometimes it is called the evening star.

Tiny planets

Pluto is the smallest planet – smaller than the Moon. It is so tiny and far away that it was not discovered until 1930. Mercury looks like the Moon. It is a round, cratered ball of rock. It has no atmosphere, so the sunny side is boiling hot, while the night side is freezing cold.

▶ If you were on Pluto, its moon, Charon, would look much larger than the Earth's Moon because Charon is very close to Pluto.

Make craters

You will need:
flour • tray • a marble or a stone

1. Spread some flour about 2 centimetres deep in a tray and smooth over the surface.

2. Drop a marble or a small round stone onto the flour and see the saucer-shaped crater that it makes.

▼ Mercury has many craters. This shows how often it was hit by space rocks. One was so large it shattered rocks on the other side of the planet.

The cratered surface of Pluto is covered in solid ice.

The Sun *looks huge as it rises over Mercury.*

Massive planets

Jupiter is the largest planet, bigger than all the other planets in the Solar System put together. It is 11 times as wide as the Earth, although it is still much smaller than the Sun. Saturn, the next largest planet, is more than nine times as wide as the Earth. Jupiter and Saturn are both gas giants. They have no solid surface and all you can see are clouds.

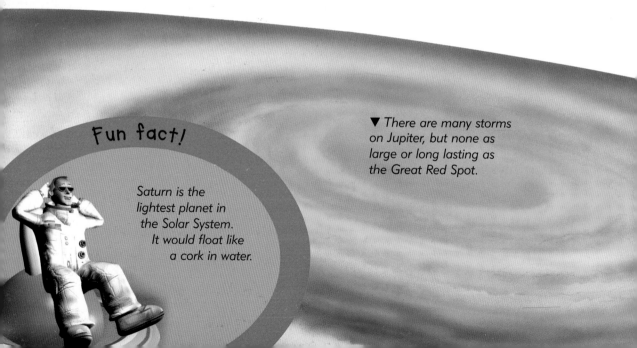

Fun fact!

Saturn is the lightest planet in the Solar System. It would float like a cork in water.

▼ There are many storms on Jupiter, but none as large or long lasting as the Great Red Spot.

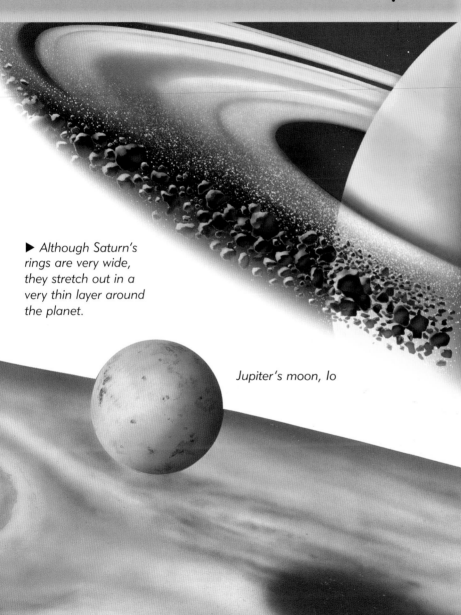

▶ Although Saturn's rings are very wide, they stretch out in a very thin layer around the planet.

Jupiter's moon, Io

Saturn's shining rings are made of millions of chunks of ice.

The Great Red Spot on Jupiter is a 300-year-old storm!

Jupiter's moon, Io, has many active volcanoes.

Far, far away

Uranus and Neptune are gas giants like Jupiter and Saturn. They are the next two planets beyond Saturn but much smaller – less than half as wide. Their surfaces are not solid, but made of liquid and gas. Their cloud tops make Uranus and Neptune look blue.

▶ Like all the gas giants, Neptune is surrounded by rings.

Neptune

▼ Most planets spin upright, but Uranus spins on its side. It may have been knocked over when something crashed into it millions of years ago.

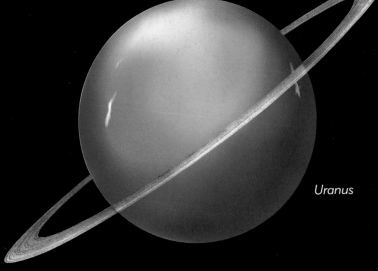

Uranus

Neptune's rings are thinner and darker than Saturn's.

Neptune's bright blue clouds make the whole planet look blue.

Uranus is very cold, being so far from the Sun.

Quiz time!

1. Which is Earth's nearest star?
2. Which is the biggest planet in our Solar System?
3. How many days are there in a year on Earth?
4. How many planets are there in the Solar System?

Answers: 1. Sun 2. Jupiter 3. 365 4. Nine

Birth of a star

A star is born in clouds of dust and gas called a nebula. Astronomers (scientists who study the stars) can see these clouds as shining patches in the night sky, or dark patches against the distant stars. These clouds shrink as gravity pulls the dust and gas together. At the centre, the gas gets hotter until a new star is born.

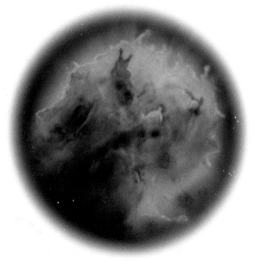

1 Clumps of gas in this nebula start to shrink into tight balls that will become stars.

2 The gas spirals as it is pulled inwards. Any leftover gas and dust may form planets around the new star.

Space

Quiz time!

1. Which is the smallest planet in the Solar System?
2. What is the name of the biggest volcano on Mars?
3. When was Pluto's moon, Charon, discovered?
4. How old is the Sun?

Answers: 1. Pluto 2. Olympus Mons 3. 1976 4. Five billion years old

Large white stars make energy very quickly and burn brightly.

4 The dust and gas are blown away and we can see the star shining. Maybe it has a family of planets like the Sun.

Small red stars are cooler and shine less brightly.

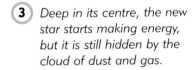

3 Deep in its centre, the new star starts making energy, but it is still hidden by the cloud of dust and gas.

The Sun has existed for five billion years – only half its life.

33

So many galaxies

The Sun is part of a huge family of stars called the Milky Way galaxy. There are billions of other stars in the galaxy and there are also billions of galaxies outside the Milky Way. Some are larger and some are smaller, but all have more stars than you can count.

Fun fact!

If you could fit the Milky Way onto these two pages, the Sun would be so small, you wouldn't be able to see it.

NASA

▼ Seen from the outside, our galaxy, the Milky Way, would look like this. We call it the Milky Way because it looks like a very faint band of light in the night sky, as though someone has spilt some milk across space.

Irregular galaxies don't have a particular shape.

Spiral galaxies have arms made of bright stars.

Galaxies that are very close pull each other out of shape.

35

Exploring the sky

People have imagined that they can see the outlines of people and animals in star patterns in the sky. These patterns are called constellations. Astronomers named the constellations to help them find their way around the skies.

► *If you live North of the Equator (the imaginary line through the centre of the Earth), these are the constellations that you can see at night.*

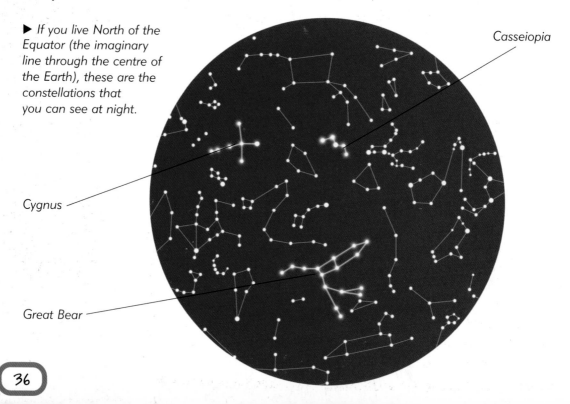

Casseiopia

Cygnus

Great Bear

The Scorpion is so-called because it looks like a scorpion.

▶ If you live south of the Equator, you can see a different set of constellations in the sky, including the Great Dog.

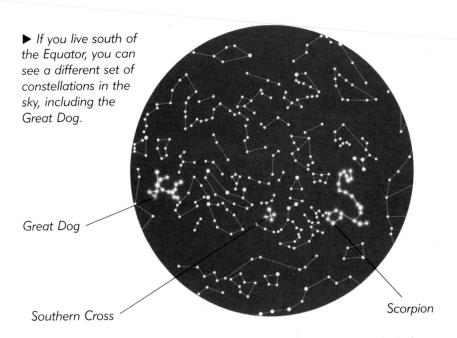

Great Dog

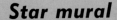

Southern Cross

Scorpion

The Great Bear is one of the best-known star formations.

The Southern Cross can be used as a compass.

Star mural

You will need:
scissors • gold and silver foil • PVA glue • glitter • black paper

1. Cut out star shapes from the gold and silver foil.

2. Stick the stars onto the black paper.

3. Cover the background with PVA and sprinkle glitter to make a sparkling Milky Way galaxy.

Launching into space

To blast into space, a rocket has to travel nearly 40 times faster than a jumbo jet. If it goes any slower, gravity pulls it back to Earth. Rockets are powered by burning fuel, which makes hot gases. These gases rush out of the engines, shooting the rocket forwards.

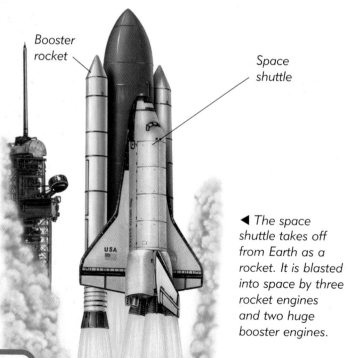

Booster rocket

Space shuttle

◀ The space shuttle takes off from Earth as a rocket. It is blasted into space by three rocket engines and two huge booster engines.

Rocket power

You will need:

balloon

If you blow up a balloon and let it go, the balloon shoots off across the room. The air inside the balloon has rushed out, pushing the balloon away in the opposite direction. A rocket blasting into space works in a similar way.

Satellite goes
into space

③

◀ A single rocket is
not powerful enough
to launch a spacecraft
or satellite into space,
so rockets have two or
three stages.

Main rocket tank

The second stage
engines carry the
rocket further

②

Booster rockets
drop away after
two minutes

①

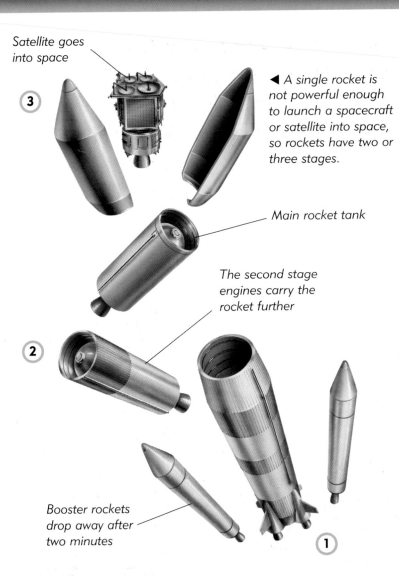

Booster rockets
give extra speed to
a spacecraft.

**The main rocket
tank** drops away
after six minutes.

Satellites need
rockets to launch
them into space.

Life in space

Space is a dangerous place for astronauts.
It can be boiling hot in the sunshine or
freezing cold in the Earth's shadow. There
is also radiation (rays of energy) from the Sun.
Dust, rocks and bits from other rockets speed
through space at such speed, they could easily
make a small hole in a spacecraft, letting the
air leak out.

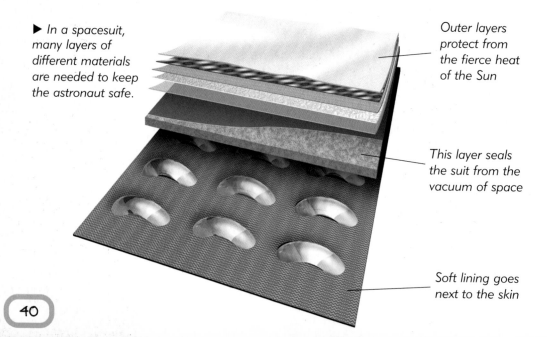

▶ In a spacesuit,
many layers of
different materials
are needed to keep
the astronaut safe.

Outer layers
protect from
the fierce heat
of the Sun

This layer seals
the suit from the
vacuum of space

Soft lining goes
next to the skin

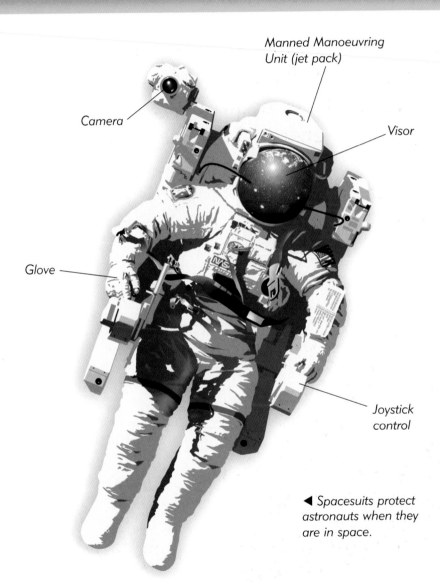

Camera

Manned Manoeuvring
Unit (jet pack)

Visor

Glove

Joystick
control

◄ Spacesuits protect
astronauts when they
are in space.

The visor
protects the
astronaut's face
from sunlight.

**The joystick
control** lets the
astronaut move
around in space.

Tubes of water
under the spacesuit
carry away heat.

41

At home in space

A space station is a home in space for astronauts and cosmonauts (Russian astronauts). It has a kitchen for making meals, cabins with sleeping bags, toilets, washbasins and sometimes showers. The space station has places to work and controls where astronauts can check that everything is working properly.

▶ *Sixteen countries are helping to build the* International Space Station, *including the US, Russia, Japan, Canada, Brazil and 11 European countries.*

Control module

Living module

The Soyuz ferry

Solar panels use sunlight to make electricity for the ISS.

The Soyuz ferry is a Russian spacecraft that takes astronauts to and from the ISS.

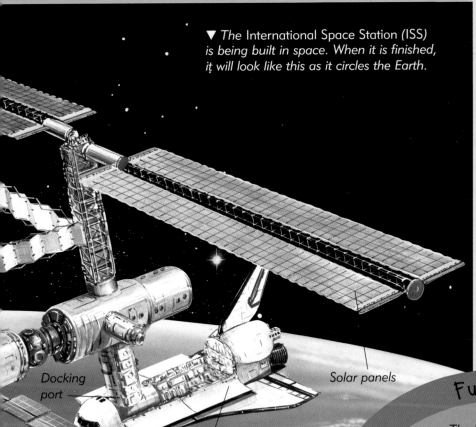

▼ The International Space Station (ISS) is being built in space. When it is finished, it will look like this as it circles the Earth.

Docking port

Solar panels

Space shuttle

Fun fact!

The US space station Skylab, launched in 1973, fell back to Earth in 1979. Most of it landed in the ocean but some pieces hit Australia.

Exploring with robots

Robot spacecraft called probes have explored all the planets except Pluto. Probes travel in space to take measurements and close-up pictures. They send the information back to scientists on Earth. Some probes circle planets taking pictures. For a close-up look, a probe can land on the surface.

▼ *In 1976, two Viking spacecraft landed on Mars to look for life, but found nothing.*

▼ *Mars Pathfinder carried a small rover called Sojourner to Mars in 1997. Sojourner spent three months on Mars, testing the soil and rocks.*

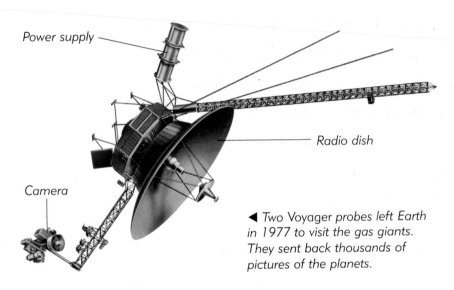

Power supply

Radio dish

Camera

◀ Two Voyager probes left Earth in 1977 to visit the gas giants. They sent back thousands of pictures of the planets.

Probes have their own power supply to explore the planets.

Cameras on a probe take detailed pictures of a planet.

Radio dishes send messages back to Earth.

Quiz time!

1. How much does the Earth weigh?
2. What is a group of stars called?
3. What does ISS stand for?
4. What is the Southern Cross?

Answers: **1.** 6000 million million million tonnes **2.** Galaxy **3.** International Space Station **4.** Constellation south of the Equator

Spies in space

Hundreds of satellites circle the Earth in space. They are used for communication, checking the weather, making maps and finding out more about space.

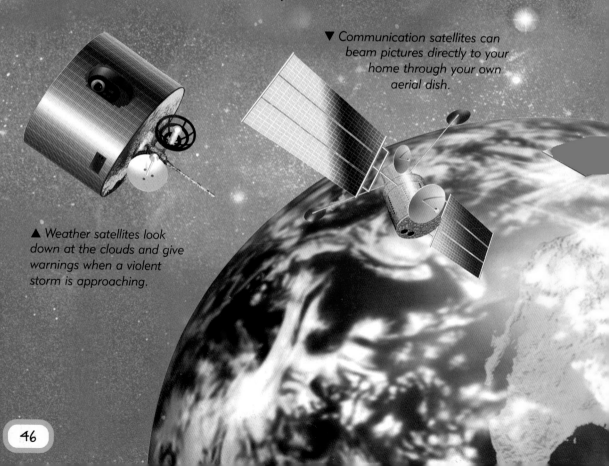

▼ Communication satellites can beam pictures directly to your home through your own aerial dish.

▲ Weather satellites look down at the clouds and give warnings when a violent storm is approaching.

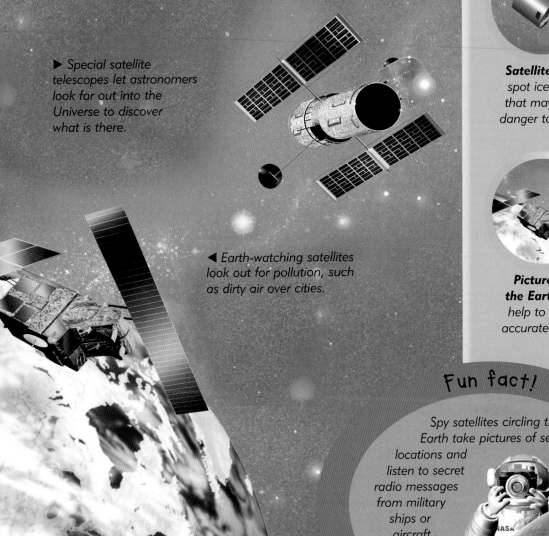

Satellites can spot icebergs that may be a danger to ships.

▶ Special satellite telescopes let astronomers look far out into the Universe to discover what is there.

◀ Earth-watching satellites look out for pollution, such as dirty air over cities.

Pictures of the Earth can help to make accurate maps.

Fun fact!

Spy satellites circling the Earth take pictures of secret locations and listen to secret radio messages from military ships or aircraft.

Off to the Moon

The first men landed on the Moon in 1969.
Three astronauts went into space on the
US *Apollo 11* mission. Neil Armstrong was
the first person to walk on the Moon. Only
five other *Apollo* missions have landed on
the Moon since then.

▼ *The distance from the Earth to the Moon is nearly 400,000 kilometres. That is about as far as travelling round the Earth ten times.*

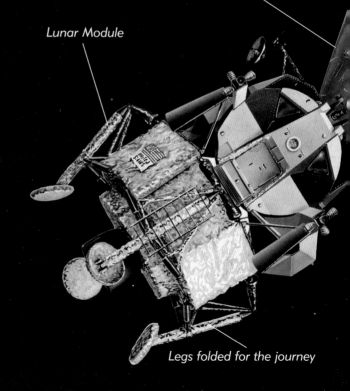

Command Module

Lunar Module

Legs folded for the journey

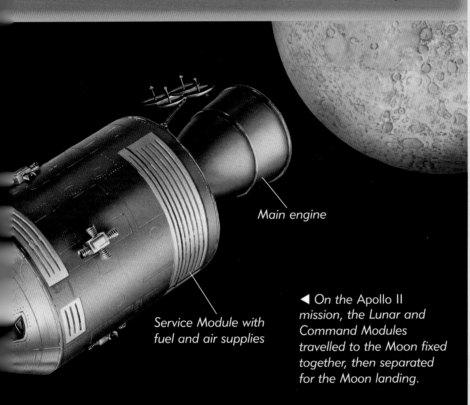

Main engine

Service Module with
fuel and air supplies

◀ On the Apollo II
mission, the Lunar and
Command Modules
travelled to the Moon fixed
together, then separated
for the Moon landing.

Moon watch

You will need:
paper • ruler • pens

1. Divide a sheet of paper into squares for the days of the month.

2. Each night draw the shape of the Moon as you see it.

3. Don't forget, when it's a new Moon, you won't see anything
   so just draw a dark sky.

The Lunar Module
took two astronauts
to the surface of
the Moon.

**The Command
Module** was the
same size as a car.

**The longest
time** spent on
the Moon was
three days.

Planet Earth

The Earth is a living planet, with water, air, plants and animals. It is covered by amazing natural features, such as mighty rivers, vast deserts and lands of ice and snow. Read about why volcanoes erupt, how earthquakes happen and why there are mountains under the ocean.

Forming the Earth

Scientists think that around 4500 million years ago the Earth formed from a huge cloud of gas and dust. A star near the cloud exploded, making the cloud spin. Gases gathered at the centre of the cloud and made the Sun. Rocks crashed into each other making the planets. The Earth is one of these planets.

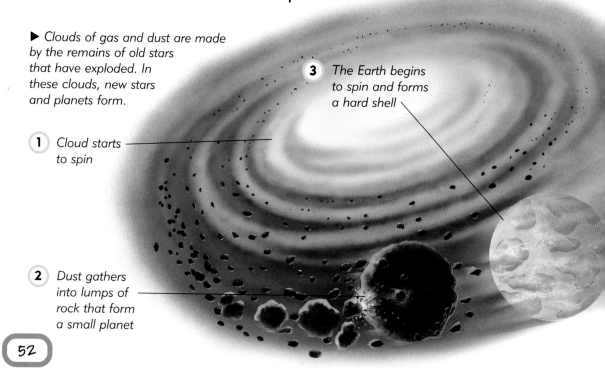

▶ Clouds of gas and dust are made by the remains of old stars that have exploded. In these clouds, new stars and planets form.

1 Cloud starts to spin

2 Dust gathers into lumps of rock that form a small planet

3 The Earth begins to spin and forms a hard shell

5 *In the beginning, the Earth was made up of one piece of land. It is now split into seven chunks called continents*

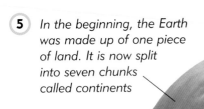

Erupting volcanoes *and fierce storms helped to form the atmosphere.*

The Moon *was hit by rocks that made round hollows, called craters.*

Fun fact!

Millions of rocks crash into the Earth as it speeds through space. The larger ones that reach the ground are called meteorites.

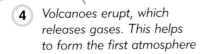

4 *Volcanoes erupt, which releases gases. This helps to form the first atmosphere*

Inside the Earth

There are different parts to the Earth.
There is a thin, rocky crust, a solid
middle called the mantle and
a centre called the core.
The outer part of the
core is liquid, but the
inner core is made
of solid metal.

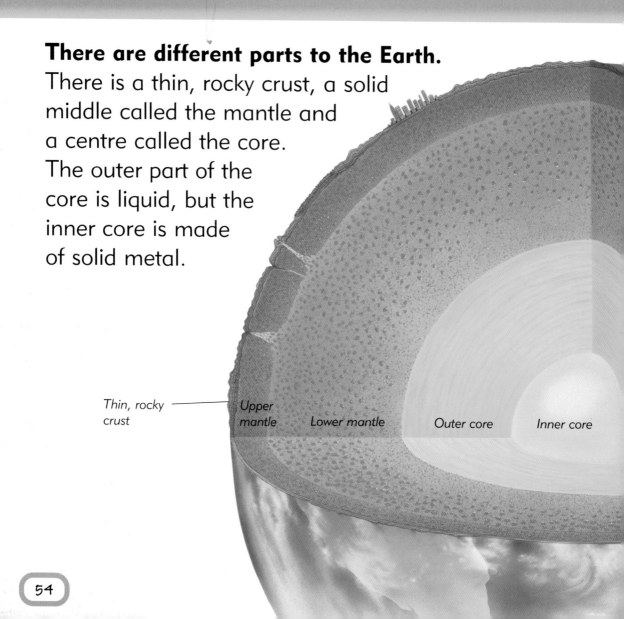

Thin, rocky
crust

Upper
mantle

Lower mantle

Outer core

Inner core

Quiz time!

1. How many continents are there?
2. What are rocks from space that hit the Earth called?
3. What helped form the Earth's atmosphere?

Answers: 1. Seven 2. Meteorites 3. Volcanoes

The continental crust is about 20 to 70 kilometres thick.

The inner core is very hot – 15 million degrees Celsius!

Molten rock can burst through the crust, creating volcanoes.

◄ If the Earth could be cut open, this is what you would see inside. It has layers inside it, like an onion.

Spinning around

▶ It is daytime when one part of the Earth faces the Sun. At the same time on the opposite side of the Earth, it is night-time.

Mid-day

Sun

Evening

The Earth is like a huge spinning top. It continues to spin because it was formed from a spinning cloud of gas and dust. It does not spin straight up like a top but leans a little to one side. The Earth takes 24 hours to spin around once. This period of time is called a day.

The Earth spins around two points – the North Pole and the South Pole.

When the Sun, Earth and Moon line up, it is called an eclipse.

The Sun's rays take 8 minutes and 20 seconds to reach the Earth.

Morning

Day and night

You will need:
globe of the Earth • torch

1. In a darkened room, shine the torch at your globe. The side facing the torch (or Sun) is lit up, so there it is daytime. On the dark side of the globe it is night-time.

2. If you slowly spin the globe round, you will see how daylight moves around the Earth.

◀ The Earth moves around the Sun in a path called an orbit. It takes one year to make this journey. In that time it spins nearly 365 ¼ times.

Night

Rocks can change

When a rock forms in the Earth's crust, it may soon be changed again. There are two main ways this can happen. In one way, the rock is heated by hot rocks moving up through the crust. In another way, the crust is squashed and heated, and mountains form.

▶ There are many layers of rock underground. They can be changed by heat and movement.

The rock dips down away from the coast to make the deep ocean

Layers of rock beneath the sea

Some hot rock travels to the surface through the pipe in a volcano

Squashed rock can become folded

Breccia is made of rocks stuck together with natural cements.

Limestone is white, yellow or greyish in colour. It is a soft rock.

Most chalk formed millions of years ago.

Quiz time!

1. What is the centre of the Earth called?
2. How thick is the Earth's crust?
3. How hot is the Sun's core?
4. When the Earth, Sun and Moon line up, what is it called?

Answers: 1. Core **2.** 20 to 70 kilometres **3.** 5 million degrees Celsius **4.** Eclipse

Violent volcanoes

Volcanoes occur when hot, liquid rock shoots up through the Earth's surface.
Beneath a volcano is a huge space filled with molten (liquid) rock. This is the magma chamber. Eruptions happen when pressure builds up inside the chamber.

▶ When a volcano erupts, the hot rock from inside the Earth escapes as ash, smoke, flying lumps called volcanic bombs, and rivers of lava.

Make your own volcano

You will need:
bicarbonate of soda • plastic bottle
red food colouring • vinegar • sand • tray

1. Put a tablespoon of bicarbonate of soda in the plastic bottle.

2. Stand the bottle on a tray and make a cone of sand around it.

3. Put a few drops of red food colouring in half a cup of vinegar.

4. Pour the vinegar into the bottle and watch your volcano erupt!

Magma cooling down under the volcano

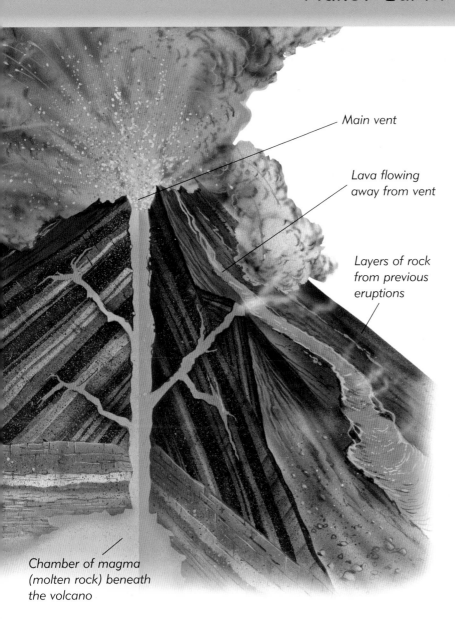

Main vent

Lava flowing
away from vent

Layers of rock
from previous
eruptions

Chamber of magma
(molten rock) beneath
the volcano

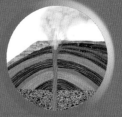

Shield volcanoes
form when lava
flows from the
vent creating a
dome shape.

**Cone-shaped
volcanoes** form
when ash settles
on thick lava.

Crater volcanoes
form when
cone-shaped
volcanoes sink into
magma chambers.

Making mountains

It takes millions of years for mountains to form.
A group of mountains is called a range. Young
mountains are the highest – they have uneven
peaks because soft rocks on the mountain tops
break down easily. Underneath are harder rocks
that take longer to break down, but even these
are worn away in time.

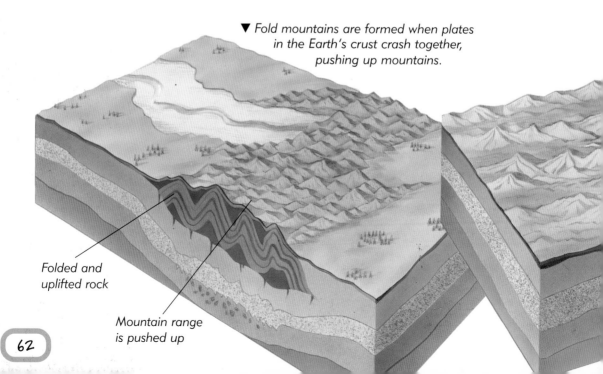

▼ Fold mountains are formed when plates
in the Earth's crust crash together,
pushing up mountains.

Folded and
uplifted rock

Mountain range
is pushed up

Planet Earth

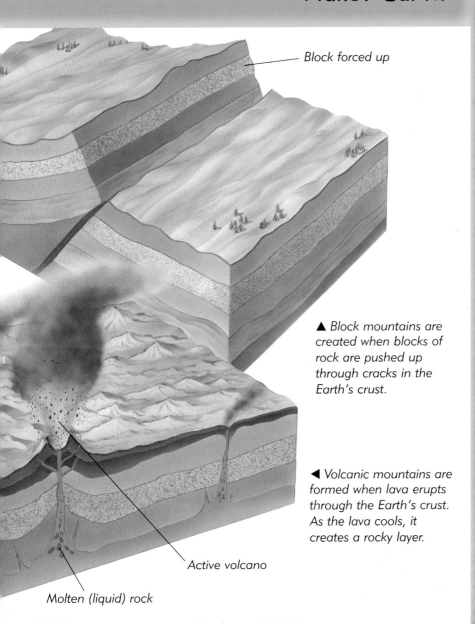

Block forced up

▲ Block mountains are created when blocks of rock are pushed up through cracks in the Earth's crust.

◀ Volcanic mountains are formed when lava erupts through the Earth's crust. As the lava cools, it creates a rocky layer.

Active volcano

Molten (liquid) rock

Some mountains are so tall that their peaks are hidden by cloud.

A crack in the Earth's crust is called a fault.

Layers of ash and lava build up to form volcanic mountains.

Shaking and quaking

An earthquake is caused by movements in the Earth's crust. An earthquake starts deep underground at the focus. Shock waves move from the focus in all directions, shaking the rock. The earthquake is strongest at the epicentre (where the shock waves reach the surface).

▶ *Earthquakes can make buildings collapse and cause cracks in roads.*

Earthquake key

1. *Focus*
2. *Shock waves from the focus*
3. *Epicentre*
4. *Fault line*

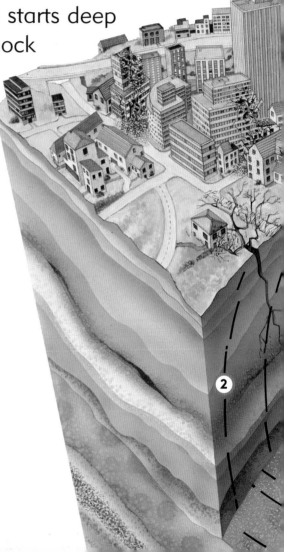

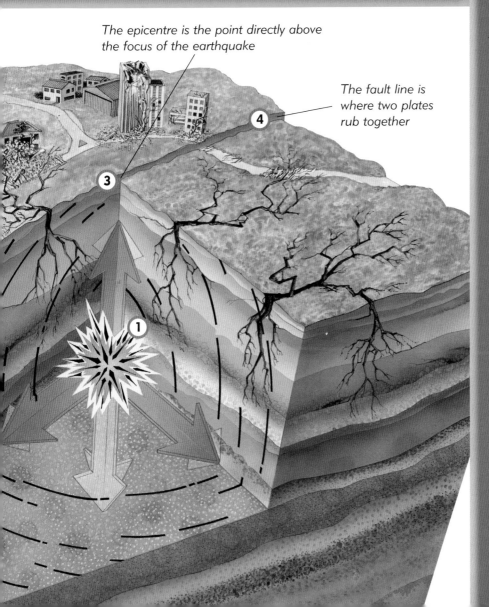

The epicentre is the point directly above the focus of the earthquake

The fault line is where two plates rub together

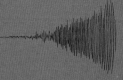

Shock waves from earthquakes are measured using the Richter Scale.

The focus is deep underground – this is where the earthquake starts.

At level 7 of the Richter Scale, buildings collapse.

65

Lakes and rivers

A mighty river can start from a spring.
This is a place where water flows from the
ground. Rain soaks into the ground through
the soil and rock, until it gushes out on the side
of a hill. The trickle of water from a spring is
called a stream. When streams join
together, they make a river.

Oxbow lakes form when meanders
separate from the main river

Meanders are loops
made by a river as it
winds down to the sea

A delta is a group of
sandy islands at the
mouth of a river

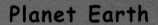

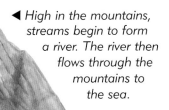

◀ *High in the mountains, streams begin to form a river. The river then flows through the mountains to the sea.*

Landslides *can fall into rivers and block the flow of water, forming lakes.*

Lakes can form *inside craters of volcanoes.*

Fun fact!

Most lakes are just blue, but some are green, pink, red or even white! The colours are made by tiny creatures called algae or by minerals in the water.

Under the surface

When rain falls on limestone, it can form caves. Rainwater can mix with carbon dioxide (a gas) to form an acid strong enough to attack limestone and make it dissolve. Underground, the rainwater makes caves in which streams and lakes can be found. In wet weather, the caves may even flood.

▶ Water flows through the cracks in limestone and makes them wider, forming caves. The horizontal caves are called galleries and the vertical caves are called shafts.

Waterfall
in a shaft

Gallery

Stalactite

Stalagmite

Waterfall in
a sink hole

Stalactites grow
down from the
roof of caves.

Stalagmites grow
up from the floor
of caves. They are
made of the
minerals in water.

Fun fact!

Stalactites grow
from the ceiling of
a cave. Stalagmites
grow from the floor
– but over time, they
can join together!

Lands of sand

The driest places on Earth are deserts. In many deserts there is a short period of rain every year, but some deserts have dry weather for many years. There are six main deserts in the world.

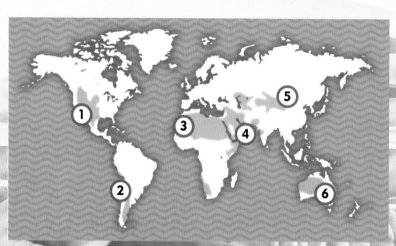

Desert key

① Great Basin and Mojave

② Atacama

③ Sahara

④ Arabian

⑤ Gobi

⑥ Great Sandy, Gibson, Great Victoria, Simpson

1. What scale measures the shock waves of earthquakes?
2. How many main deserts are there in the world?
3. What is molten rock also known as?
4. Where does an earthquake start?

Answers: 1. Richter Scale **2.** Six **3.** Magma **5.** Underground, at the focus

▼ An oasis is a pool of water in the desert. It forms when rainwater collects in the rock beneath the sand, and then moves up to the surface.

Ridges of sand are blown by strong winds into dunes.

Camels have broad feet that stop them sinking in the sand.

In the desert it can be as hot as 50 degrees Celsius in the daytime.

71

Forests of the world

There are three main types of forest. In coniferous forests, the trees stay in leaf all year round. Trees lose their leaves in winter and grow new ones in spring in temperate woodland. Rainforests have thick vegetation and lots of rainfall.

▼ *Deciduous trees lose their leaves in winter and grow new leaves in spring. They are found in temperate forests.*

▲ The clouded leopard lives in the forests of Southeast Asia. It has a long tail, which helps it to balance when climbing trees.

Guessing game

Can you guess what these woodland creatures are?

1.

2.

3.

Answers: 1. Deer 2. Badger 3. Woodpecker

Millions of insects live in rainforests, including butterflies.

Squirrels live in both temperate and coniferous forests.

Coniferous trees grow where winters are very cold.

Water, water everywhere

Oceans cover over two-thirds of the Earth's rocky surface. Their total area is about 362 million square kilometres, which means there is more than twice as much ocean than land!

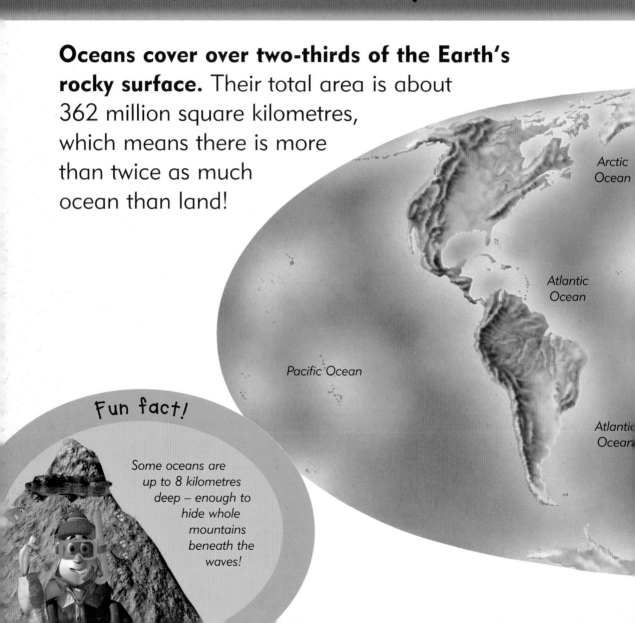

Arctic Ocean

Atlantic Ocean

Pacific Ocean

Atlantic Ocean

Fun fact!

Some oceans are up to 8 kilometres deep – enough to hide whole mountains beneath the waves!

Planet Earth

▼ Although all the oceans flow into each other, we know them as four different oceans – the Pacific, Atlantic, Indian and Arctic. Each ocean is made up of smaller areas of water called seas.

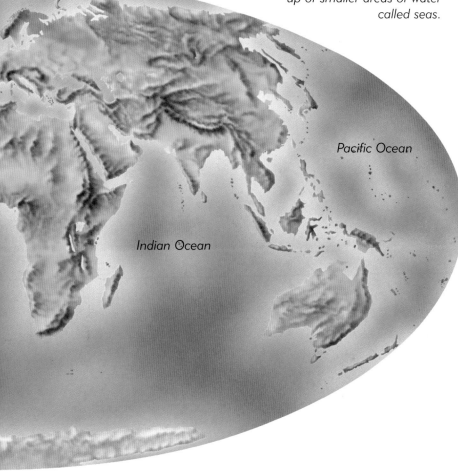

Pacific Ocean

Indian Ocean

***In its deepest parts**, the Pacific Ocean would cover Mount Everest.*

***Ocean waves** carve into rocks creating shapes such as sea stacks.*

***Icebergs** break away from huge glaciers and then drift and melt into the oceans.*

Under the ocean

There are plains, mountains and valleys under the ocean, in areas called basins. Each basin has a rim (the flat continental shelf that meets the shore) and sides (the continental slope that drops away from the shelf). As the ocean floor is slowly moving, its features are always changing.

▶ Under the ocean there is a landscape similar to that found on land. There are flat plains, steep hills, huge underwater volcanoes and deep valleys.

Volcanic island

Ocean trench (deep valley)

Planet Earth

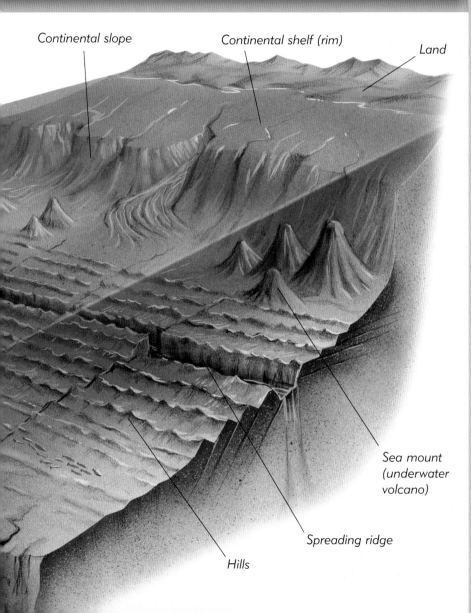

Continental slope

Continental shelf (rim)

Land

Sea mount
(underwater
volcano)

Spreading ridge

Hills

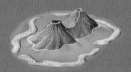

Stage 1
A coral reef may
build up around
a volcanic island.

Stage 2
The volcanic island
sinks, leaving a
lagoon – water that
is separate from
the main ocean.

Stage 3
An atoll is the
ring of coral
reef surrounding
the lagoon.

Rock pool life

Rock pools are full of many living things, including limpets, sponges, anemones, fish and plants. They eat scraps of food that are washed in with the tide. These pools are also the perfect hiding place for creatures, such as crabs.

Rock pool key

1. Anemone
2. Starfish
3. Limpets
4. Fish
5. Shrimp
6. Hermit crab
7. Sponge

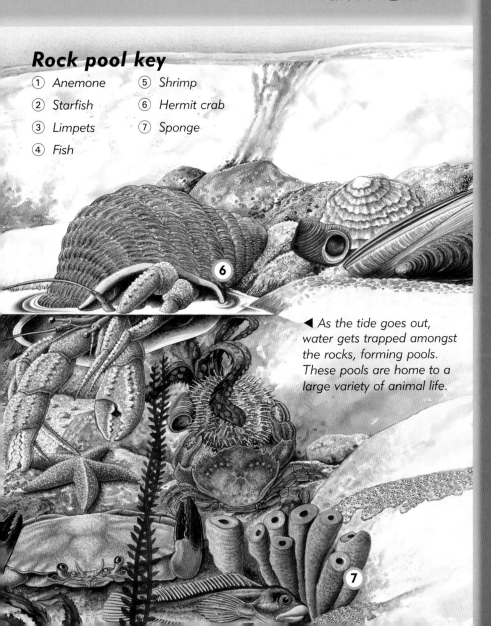

◀ As the tide goes out, water gets trapped amongst the rocks, forming pools. These pools are home to a large variety of animal life.

Sponges are simple animals that filter food from sea water.

Hermit crabs live in shells that are left behind by other sea creatures.

Starfish can lose an arm if attacked, but they are able to grow a new one.

79

Tropical life

Tiny animals build huge underwater walls.
The walls are built up from coral – the leftover
skeletons of sea creatures called polyps. Over
millions of years, enough skeletons pile up to
form huge, structures called reefs. Coral
reefs are full of colourful sea life.

▶ The creatures found in
coral reefs are very colourful.
This helps them to blend with
their surroundings, making it
hard for hunters to spot them.

1

2

3

4

Coral reef key

1. Sea horse
2. Parrot fish
3. Giant clam
4. Sea anemone
5. Cleaner wrasse fish
6. Clownfish
7. Lion fish
8. Stone fish

Giant clams are shellfish that can grow up to one metre long!

Baby sea horses stream out of their father's pouch into the sea.

Clownfish swim unharmed amongst the tentacles of sea anemones.

81

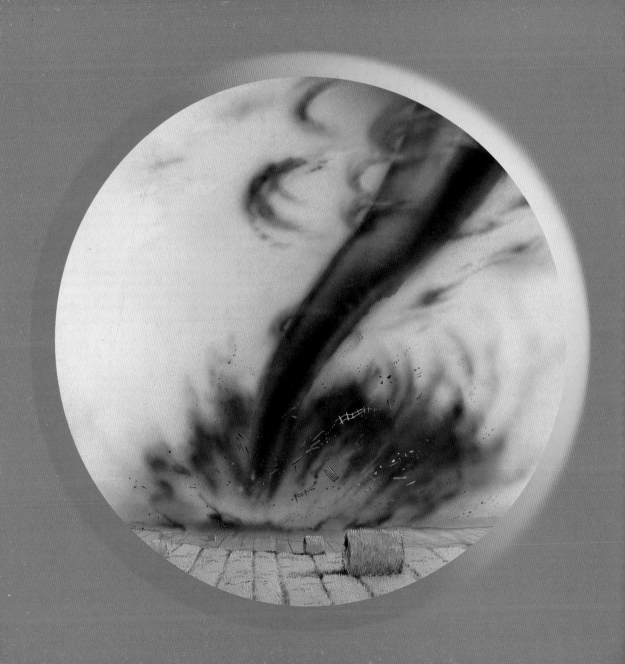

Weather

Weather is all around us – rain, wind, sunshine or snow. It changes all the time and can affect many things, such as how animals and plants survive. Discover how a thunderstorm happens, what snow is made of, and why tornadoes and hurricanes are so dangerous.

Layers of air

Our planet is wrapped in a blanket of air called the atmosphere. It stretches for hundreds of kilometres above our heads. The blanket keeps in heat, especially at night when part of the planet faces away from the Sun. During the day, it becomes a sunscreen instead. Without an atmosphere, there would be no weather.

◀ The higher up you go, the less oxygen there is in the air. We need oxygen to breathe, so mountaineers often wear special breathing equipment.

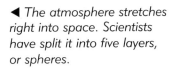

◀ *The atmosphere stretches right into space. Scientists have split it into five layers, or spheres.*

Exosphere
190 to 960 kilometres

Thermosphere
80 to 190 kilometres

Mesosphere
50 to 80 kilometres

Stratosphere
10 to 50 kilometres

Troposphere
0 to 10 kilometres

Low-level satellites *orbit within the outer layers of the atmosphere.*

Meteorites *are pieces of rock from space.*

Mountaineers *wear masks that help them to breathe in more oxygen.*

85

What is weather?

Rain, sunshine, snow and storms are all types of weather. The weather is caused by what is happening in the atmosphere – the blanket of air that surrounds the Earth. In parts of the world, such as near the Equator, the weather is nearly always the same. Most of the world has a temperate climate, meaning the weather changes daily.

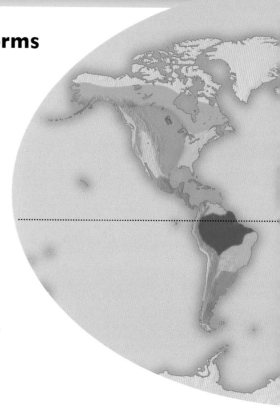

Desert

Mountainous

Tropical forest

Cold temperate

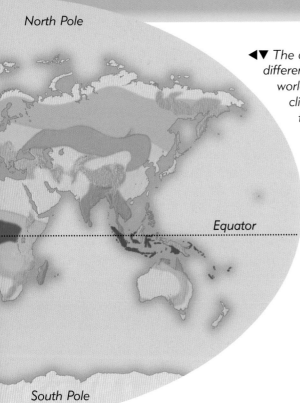

North Pole

Equator

South Pole

◀▼ *The coloured rings show the different climates around the world. In general, the warmest climates are found close to the Equator.*

Tropical grassland

Temperate grassland

Dry temperate

Wet temperate

Polar

Most of the world has a temperate climate – it is neither too hot nor too cold.

Near the North and South Poles, there is a cold, polar climate.

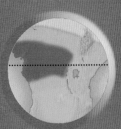

The Equator is an imaginary line around the middle of the Earth.

Guessing the weather

Working out what the weather will be like is called forecasting. By looking at changes in the atmosphere, and comparing them to weather patterns of the past, forecasters can make an accurate guess at what the weather will be tomorrow, the next day, or even further ahead.

A cold front (where cold air pushes under warm air) is shown by a blue triangle

A warm front (where warm air pushes over colder air) is shown by a red semi-circle

Black lines with red semi-circles and blue triangles are where a cold front meets a warm front

These white lines are isobars – closely spaced isobars mean strong wind

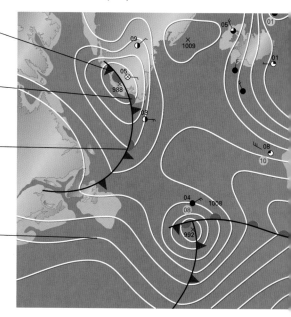

▼ Weather scientists, called meteorologists, plot their findings on maps called synoptic charts.

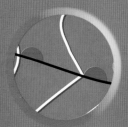

Weather symbols

Make your own synoptic chart. Here are some symbols to get you started. Can you guess what they mean?

1.

2.

3.

Answers: 1. Sun **2.** Rain and snow **3.** Cloud

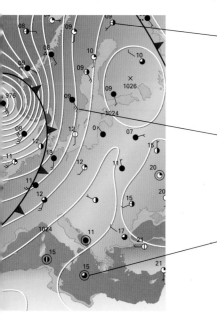

The white semi-circle shows how much cloud cover there is

The three lines on the tail show that the wind is very strong

This symbol shows an area of calm, with lots of cloud cover

A warm front is a sign of cooler weather to come.

A cold front can bring heavy rain and thunderstorms.

Weather symbols make up a common language for meteorologists.

All the seasons

There are four seasons – spring, summer, autumn and winter. They are caused by the Earth's movement around the Sun. It takes one year for the Earth to orbit around the Sun. The Earth is tilted, so over the year the North and South Pole take turns facing towards the Sun, giving us seasons.

▼ In autumn, many forests change colour, from green to golden brown. Trees prepare for the winter months by losing their leaves.

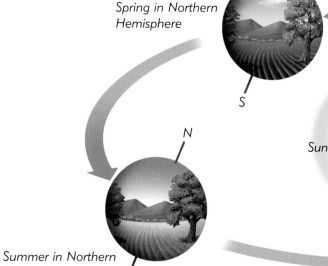

Spring in Northern Hemisphere

N

S

Summer in Northern Hemisphere

N

S

Sun

▲ At the North Pole during the height of summer, the Sun never disappears below the horizon.

Summer in the Northern Hemisphere is between June and September.

Winter in the Northern Hemisphere is between December and March.

Winter in Northern Hemisphere

N

S

◄ In June in the Northern Hemisphere, the North Pole leans towards the Sun. The Sun heats the northern half of the Earth, making it summertime.

N

Autumn in Northern Hemisphere

S

Fun fact!

In Stockholm, Sweden, the longest day lasts 21 hours because the Sun disappears below the horizon for only three hours!

Tropical seasons

Many parts of the tropics have two seasons, not four. The tropics are the parts of the world closest to the Equator. In June, tropical areas north of the Equator have the strongest heat and heaviest rains. In December, it is the turn of the areas south of the Equator.

◄ Rainforests have rainy weather all year round – but there is still a wet and dry season. It is just that the wet season is even wetter!

Weather

▶ Monsoons are winds that carry heavy rains. The rains fall in the tropics during the hot, rainy season. They can cause chaos, turning streets into rivers and even washing people's homes away.

Daily rainfall feeds the lush rainforest vegetation.

The tropics are always hot, as they are constantly facing the Sun.

▼ The tropics, shown in red, lie either side of the Equator, between lines of latitude called the Tropic of Cancer and the Tropic of Capricorn.

Tropic of Cancer

Equator

Tropic of Capricorn

Fun fact!

In parts of India, over 26,000 millimetres of rain have fallen in a single year!

Scorching Sun

All our heat comes from the Sun. The Sun is a star – a super-hot ball of burning gases. It gives off heat rays that travel 150 million kilometres through space to the Earth. Over the journey, the rays cool down, but they are still scorching hot. The surface of the Sun is 5500 degrees Celsius.

▶ The Sahara Desert in North Africa is the sunniest place on Earth. It is home to people such as the Tuareg Arabs. They wear loose clothing to keep cool.

▼ Too much sun brings drought. Without rain, the dry earth turns to dust. Strong winds blow the dry earth, causing dust storms.

Desert peoples cover their heads to protect them from the hot sun and sand.

Camels have long eyelashes to keep sand out of their eyes.

A mirage is a trick of the light and makes us see things that aren't there.

Quiz time!

1. What colour are leaves in autumn?

2. What is the name of the imaginary line that runs around the middle of the Earth?

3. What kind of climate will you find in the North Pole?

Answers: 1. Golden 2. Equator 3. Cold, polar climate

Clouds and rain

4 *Rain falls*

5 *Rainwater flows down mountains and into rivers*

3 *Water is given off by forests*

Rain comes from the sea. As the Sun heats the ocean's surface, some sea water turns into water vapour (a kind of gas) and rises into the air to form clouds. Rain falls from the clouds, some of which is soaked up by the land, but a lot finds its way back to the sea. This is the water cycle.

Make a rain gauge

You will need:

jam jar • marker pen • ruler • notebook • pen

1. Place the jam jar outside where it can collect rain.

2. Use the marker pen to mark the water level on the outside of the jar each day.

3. Keep a record of the changing levels of rainfall in a notebook.

2 Clouds form

1 Water evaporates (disappears into the air) from the sea

6 The rivers run back to the sea, and the cycle starts again

▲ The water cycle involves all the water on Earth. Water vapour rises from lakes, rivers and the sea to form clouds in the atmosphere.

Mountains can be so tall that their peaks are hidden by cloud.

Rain is made from lots of water droplets.

Clouds trap heat, making the Earth feel warmer.

97

Windy weather

Wind is moving air. Winds blow because air is constantly moving from areas of high pressure to areas of low pressure. The bigger the difference in temperature between the two areas, the faster the wind blows.

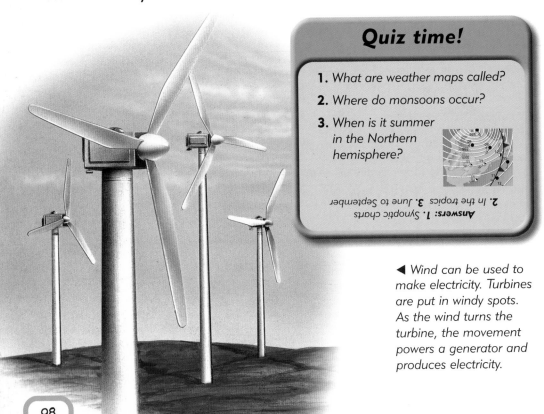

Quiz time!

1. What are weather maps called?
2. Where do monsoons occur?
3. When is it summer in the Northern hemisphere?

Answers: 1. Synoptic charts
2. In the tropics 3. June to September

◀ Wind can be used to make electricity. Turbines are put in windy spots. As the wind turns the turbine, the movement powers a generator and produces electricity.

Force 0: Calm

Force 2:
Light breeze

Force 3:
Gentle breeze

Force 4:
Moderate breeze

Force 1:
Light air

Force 5:
Fresh breeze

Force 7:
Near gale

Force 6:
Strong breeze

Force 9:
Strong gale

Force 8:
Gale

Force 10:
Storm

▶ Wind strength is measured on the Beaufort Scale. The scale ranges from Force 0, meaning total calm, to Force 12, which is a hurricane.

Force 12:
Hurricane

Force 11:
Violent storm

The Beaufort Scale is named after the Irish admiral who invented it.

The wind can be so strong, it blows trees over.

A gale can rip the tiles off a roof.

99

Thunder and lightning

Thunderstorms are most likely in summer.
Hot weather creates warm, moist air that rises
and forms tall cumulonimbus clouds. Inside
each cloud, water droplets and ice crystals
bang about, building up positive and negative
electrical charges. Electricity flows between the
charges, creating a flash that heats the air
around it – this is lightning.

▼ Lightning is so hot that it makes the
air expand (spread out), making a loud
noise or thunderclap.

How close is the storm?

Thunder and lightning happen at the same time, but light travels faster than sound, so you see the lightning first.

1. *When you see a lightning flash, count the seconds between the flash and the thunderclap that follows.*

2. *Then divide the number of seconds by three. This shows you how many kilometres away the storm is.*

3. *Keep a record and see if the storm comes when you think it will.*

Lightning that travels from the cloud to the ground is called fork lightning.

◀ *Tall buildings, such as church steeples, have lightning conductors placed on their roofs to absorb the shock.*

In some countries, hailstones can be as big as tennis balls!

▲ *Hailstones are chunks of ice that fall from thunderclouds.*

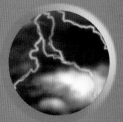

Lightning looks red if there is rain in the thundercloud.

In a spin!

A tornado forms in a thunderstorm, when the back part of the thundercloud starts spinning. The spinning air forms a funnel that reaches down towards the Earth. When it touches the ground, it becomes a tornado.

▶ A tornado spins at speeds of up to 480 kilometres an hour. It whizzes along the ground like a high-speed vacuum cleaner, sucking up everything in its path.

Waterspouts are pillars of spinning water sucked up by a tornado.

▶ Hurricane Hunters are special weather planes that fly into the storm to take measurements. This information tells us where the hurricane will go.

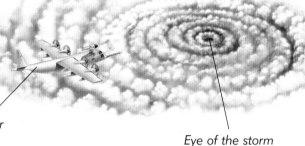

Hurricane Hunter

Eye of the storm

▼ The centre of a hurricane is calm and still. This part is called the 'eye'. As the eye of the storm passes over, there is a pause in the rains and wind.

Dust devils are desert tornadoes that create a storm of sand.

Fun fact!

Waterspouts are so strong, they can suck up fish living in a lake!

Light shows

Rainbows are caused by sunlight passing through falling raindrops. The water acts like a prism (a triangle-shaped piece of glass), which splits the light. White light is made up of seven colours – red, orange, yellow, green, blue, indigo and violet – so these are the seven colours, from top to bottom, that make up a rainbow.

◄ Rainbows are most likely to be seen towards the end of the day, especially where thunderstorms build up during hot summer days.

▲ In the far north and far south of the world, amazing patterns of light sometimes appear in the sky. These colourful curtains are called auroras. They occur when tiny particles of light from the Sun smash into the air.

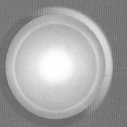

A halo looks like a circle of light around the Sun.

Mock suns are two bright spots that appear on either side of the Sun.

Fogbows happen when sunlight passes through fog.

Remember the rainbow!

Richard Of York Gave Battle In Vain

The first letter of every word of this rhyme gives the first letter of each colour of the rainbow – as it appears in the sky.

Red Orange Yellow Green Blue Indigo Violet

Science

Nearly everything around us uses science, from machines big and small, to the materials that are used to make everyday things. Discover the world of science and read about towering buildings and powerful magnets, and find out where electricity comes from.

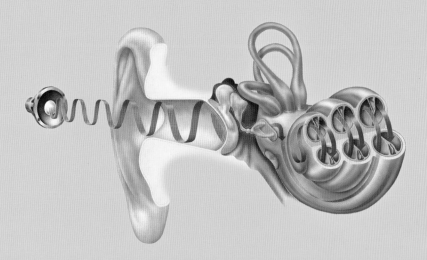

Our world of science

Why do we need science?
Science is all around us. We use science to travel and to build, we even use it to hear. Toasters, bicycles, mobile phones, cars, computers, light bulbs – all the gadgets and machines we use every day are the results of scientific discoveries.

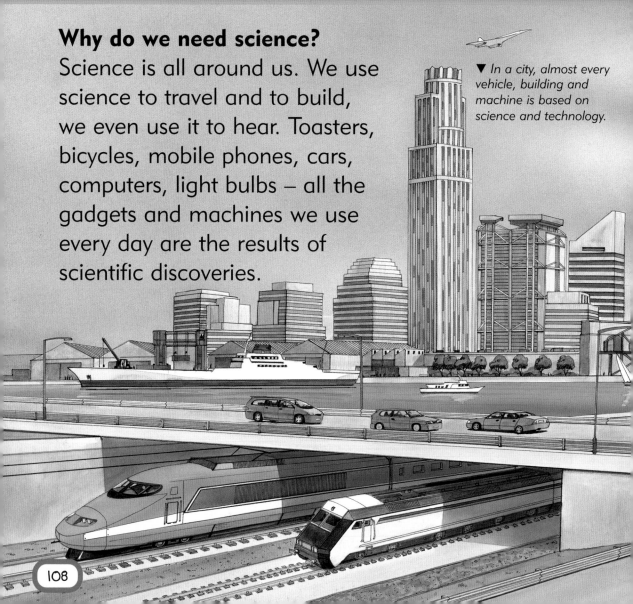

▼ In a city, almost every vehicle, building and machine is based on science and technology.

Skyscrapers are tall buildings that tower in the air.

Cranes are used to lift heavy objects.

Trains are built and powered using science.

Machines help us to do many things, or they make doing them easier. Many things around you are machines – from a see-saw in the park to the wheel on a car. Levers, screws, pulleys and wheels are all simple but useful machines.

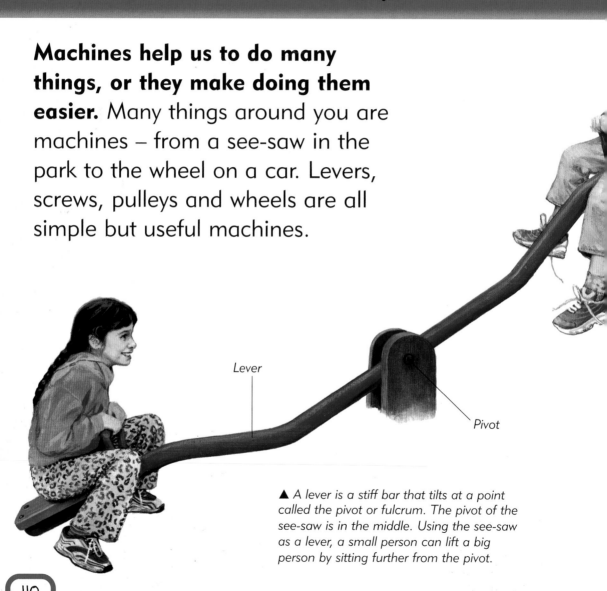

Lever

Pivot

▲ A lever is a stiff bar that tilts at a point called the pivot or fulcrum. The pivot of the see-saw is in the middle. Using the see-saw as a lever, a small person can lift a big person by sitting further from the pivot.

Science

▶ A screw is a ridge, or thread, wrapped around a bar or pole. It changes a small turning motion into a powerful pulling movement. It can be used to hold furniture together.

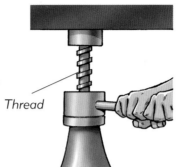

Thread

Gears can slow down or speed up the turning direction of a force.

The wheels on gears have pointed teeth around the edges.

Groove

◀ A pulley turns around like a wheel. It has a groove around its edge for a cable or rope. A pulley can be used to lift heavy weights easily.

▼ A wheel is a circular disc that turns around its centre on a bar called an axle. Wheels can carry heavy weights such as cars and trucks.

Axle

Fun fact!

A ramp is a simple machine called an inclined plane. It is easier to walk up a ramp than to jump straight to the top.

Hot science

Fire! Flames! Burning! Heat! The science of heat is important in many ways. Not only do we cook with heat, but we also warm our homes and heat water. Engines in cars, trucks and planes work by burning fuel. Even factories use heat to make steel and to shape plastics.

Carrying heat

You will need:
*wooden ruler • metal spoon • plastic spatula
heatproof jug • frozen peas • butter*

1. *Fix a frozen pea with butter to the end of the ruler, spoon and spatula.*

2. *Put the other ends in a heatproof jug. Ask an adult to fill the jug with hot water.*

3. *Heat is conducted (passed on) from the water, up the object, to melt the butter. Which object is the best conductor?*

◄ A firework is lit by a flame and burns quickly. It explodes into the air creating a loud bang!

Hot air rises from a candle. This movement of heat is called convection.

A hot drink passes its heat to the spoon, warming it up. Heat moves by conduction.

A thermometer is used for measuring heat.

Light at work

Almost everything you do relies on light and the science of light, which is called optics. Light is a form of energy that you can see. Light waves are made of electricity and magnetism – and they are tiny. About 2000 of them laid end to end would stretch across this full stop.

White light

Prism

Spectrum

Fun fact!

Light is the fastest thing in the Universe. It travels through space at 300,000 kilometres a second.

▲ When white light passes through a prism (a triangular piece of glass), it splits into seven colours. These colours are called the spectrum.

▼ Light waves bounce off surfaces that are smooth, such as a mirror. This is called reflection.

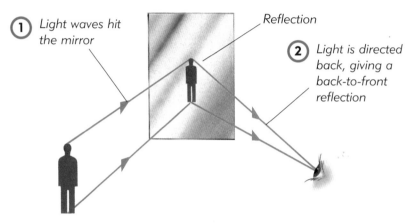

(1) Light waves hit the mirror

Reflection

(2) Light is directed back, giving a back-to-front reflection

Red, green and blue are primary colours of light.

As light passes through this glass of water, it refracts (bends) and makes the straw look bent.

Shades of colour

You will need:
Different-coloured paints • paintbrush
pen • paper

1. Mix two different colours of paint together.

2. Write down what colours you mix and what colour they make.

3. Paint a picture using your new colours.

Cameras make pictures by using lenses and light.

What a noise!

Listening to the radio or television, playing music, and shouting all depend on the science of sound – acoustics. Sounds are like invisible waves in the air. These waves travel about 330 metres a second. This is one million times slower than light waves.

(1) *Noise travels to the ear*

Box guitar

You will need:
shoebox • elastic band • split pins • card

1. Cut a hole about 10 centimetres across on one side of an empty shoebox.

2. Push split pins through either side of the hole, and stretch an elastic band between them.

3. Pluck the band. Hear how the air vibrates inside the box – like a guitar.

Loudness is measured in decibels (dB). A quiet sound, such as whispering, is about 20 dB.

A fast-moving express train is about 80 dB.

A jet plane taking off is 120 dB. This is so loud it could damage your eardrums.

(3) Tiny bones carry vibrations

(4) Vibrations travel to the cochlea (fluid-filled chamber)

(5) Sound waves vibrate through the fluid in the cochlea and travel to the brain

(2) Eardrum vibrates

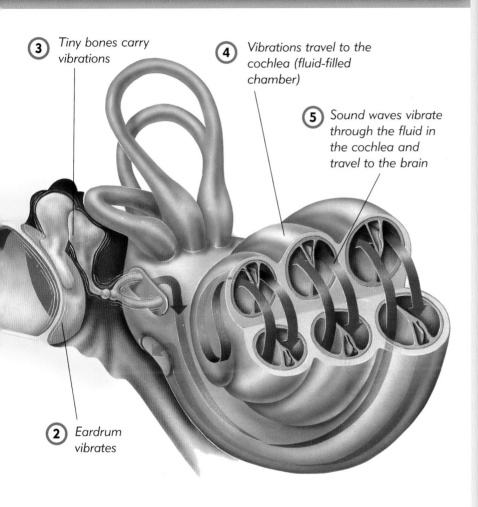

▲ We cannot see sound waves but we can hear them using our ears. Sound waves travel to the ear and then to our brain.

Magnet power

Without magnets there would be no computers, loudspeakers or electric motors. Magnetism is an invisible force to do with atoms – tiny particles that make up everything. Atoms are made of even smaller particles, including electrons. Magnetism is linked to the way that these electrons line up and move. Most magnetic substances contain iron.

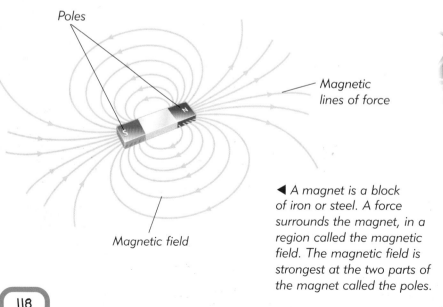

Poles

Magnetic lines of force

Magnetic field

◀ A magnet is a block of iron or steel. A force surrounds the magnet, in a region called the magnetic field. The magnetic field is strongest at the two parts of the magnet called the poles.

◀ *An electromagnet uses electricity to make it attract (pull) the body of a car.*

A magnet has two different poles – north and south.

Electromagnets are so strong they can lift whole cars.

A car's body is made from iron-based steel, which is magnetic.

119

What is electricity?

Electricity is a form of energy that flows from a power station to our home. It is used all around us to power washing machines, vacuum cleaners and kettles. Electricity is made by the movement of electrons inside atoms.

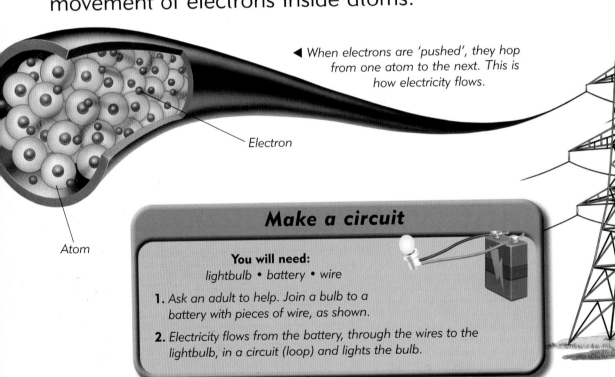

◀ When electrons are 'pushed', they hop from one atom to the next. This is how electricity flows.

Electron

Atom

Make a circuit

You will need:
lightbulb • battery • wire

1. Ask an adult to help. Join a bulb to a battery with pieces of wire, as shown.

2. Electricity flows from the battery, through the wires to the lightbulb, in a circuit (loop) and lights the bulb.

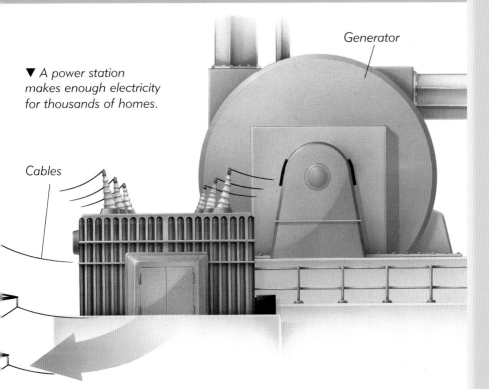

Generator

▼ A power station makes enough electricity for thousands of homes.

Cables

Pylon

▶ A battery makes electricity from chemicals. Two different chemicals next to each other, such as an acid and a metal, swap electrons, making the electricity flow.

The generator gives the 'push' that starts the electrons flowing.

Cables carry electricity into thousands of homes.

Pylons hold cables safely above the ground.

121

Invisible waves

The air is full of waves we cannot see or hear, unless we have the right machine. Radio waves are a form of electrical and magnetic energy, just like heat and light waves, microwaves and X-rays. They all travel at an equal speed – the speed of light.

Sometimes radio waves may be sent by a satellite in space

Radio waves

Aerial

▶ *Radio waves are used for both radio and television. They travel long distances from a satellite to your home, car or workplace.*

A radio picks up radio waves using its long aerial or antenna and converts them to sound waves

122

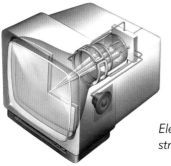

◀ Inside a TV set, the radio waves are changed into electrical signals. These make the pictures and sounds.

An electron gun fires streams of electrons

Electron stream

Three colours of dots join to make up the other colours on a TV screen.

▲ A TV screen is coated with tiny coloured dots inside. When electrons hit the dots, they glow and make the picture.

A satellite dish on the outside of a house picks up radio waves for TV channels

Fun fact!

Radio waves travel easily though space, but they hardly pass at all through water.

Computer science

Computers are amazing machines. We give them instructions and information, in various ways. These include typing on a keyboard, inserting a disc, using a joystick, or linking up a camera, scanner or another computer.

Main computer case

Microchips on circuit board

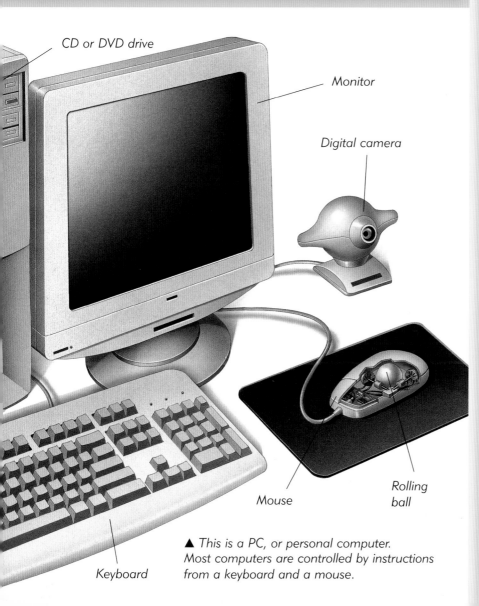

CD or DVD drive

Monitor

Digital camera

Mouse

Rolling ball

Keyboard

▲ This is a PC, or personal computer. Most computers are controlled by instructions from a keyboard and a mouse.

Microchips are the main 'brain' of a computer.

The mouse moves a pointer around the screen.

The disc drive stores information on CD or DVD.

Laser power

Laser light is a special kind of light. As with ordinary light, it is made of waves, but there are differences. For example, ordinary white light is a mixture of colours. Laser light is just one pure colour. Also, an ordinary light beam spreads and fades. A laser beam does not. It can travel for thousands of kilometres as a strong, straight beam.

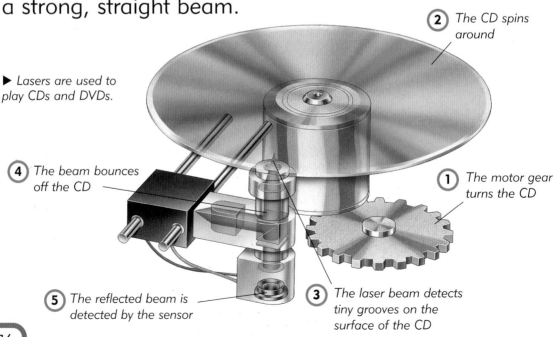

▶ Lasers are used to play CDs and DVDs.

2 The CD spins around

4 The beam bounces off the CD

1 The motor gear turns the CD

5 The reflected beam is detected by the sensor

3 The laser beam detects tiny grooves on the surface of the CD

Quiz time!

1. *What is ordinary light from the Sun called?*
2. *What do decibels (dB) measure?*
3. *How many colours of the spectrum are there?*
4. *Optics are the science of what?*

Answers: 1. White light 2. Loudness 3. Seven 4. Light

▼ *An industrial laser is used in factories for cutting and melting metal.*

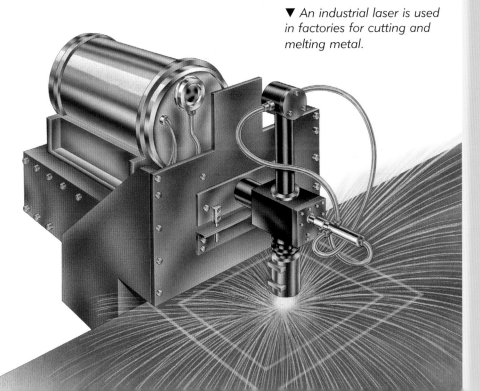

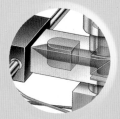

Lasers *were invented in 1960 by Dr Maiman.*

CDs and DVDs *are used to play music and films.*

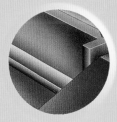

Industrial lasers *have the power to cut a neat line through metal.*

Amazing web

The world is at your fingertips – if you are on the Internet. The Internet is one of the most amazing results of modern-day science. It is a worldwide network of computers, linked like one huge electrical spider's web.

A modem changes telephone signals to computer signals

Email is a quick way of sending messages to other Internet users

▲ The web spans the world as signals of electricity, radio, light and microwaves. The Internet is all the computers and all the links that use the World Wide Web.

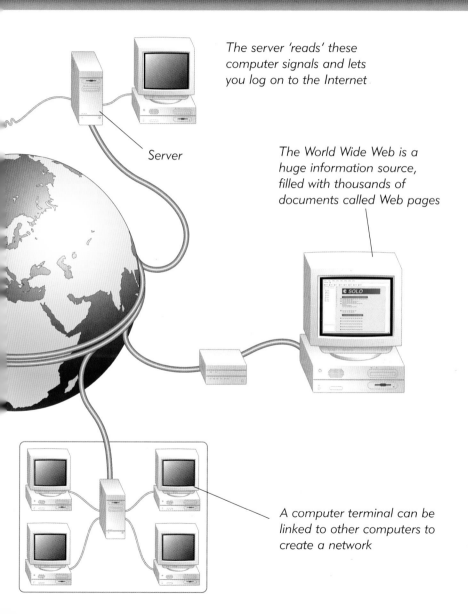

The server 'reads' these computer signals and lets you log on to the Internet

Server

The World Wide Web is a huge information source, filled with thousands of documents called Web pages

A computer terminal can be linked to other computers to create a network

A website is like an electronic version of a leaflet or book.

Telephone wires carry signals from computer to computer.

Email means electronic mail – sending messages over the Internet.

What is it made of?

You would not make a bridge out of straw, or a cup out of thin paper. Choosing the right material for a job is part of materials science. All substances can be divided into several groups. The biggest group is metals, such as iron and silver. Most metals are strong and carry heat and electricity well. They are used where materials must be tough and long-lasting.

The main body of the car is made from carbon fibre – a light but very strong material. This makes the car go faster, but protects it from damage

The car's axles are made from titanium – a very strong, light metal. They help reduce the weight of the car

Quiz time!

1. When were lasers invented?
2. What group of substances do iron and silver belong to?
3. What is the main body of a racing car made out of?
4. What are mixtures of different substances called?

Answers: **1.** 1960 **2.** Metals **3.** Carbon fibre **4.** Composites

◀ A racing car has thousands of parts made from hundreds of materials. Each is suited to certain conditions such as stress, temperature and vibrations.

The engine can produce about ten times as much power as an ordinary car – but it needs to be as light as possible

Composites are mixtures of different materials, such as fibre and ceramic.

Fibre is a threadlike substance, such as nylon or cotton.

Ceramics are made from clay or other substances dug from the Earth.

Atoms are the smallest bits of a substance.
They are so tiny, even a billion atoms would
be too small to see. Scientists have carried
out experiments to find out what is inside
an atom. The answer is – even smaller
bits. These are subatomic particles, and
there are three main kinds – protons,
neutrons and electrons. Each substance has
its own number of protons and neutrons.

▶ *The centre of each atom is called the nucleus.*
Electrons whizz round the nucleus.

Fun fact!

Atoms are so
small that a grain
of sand, contains
at least 100 billion
billion atoms!

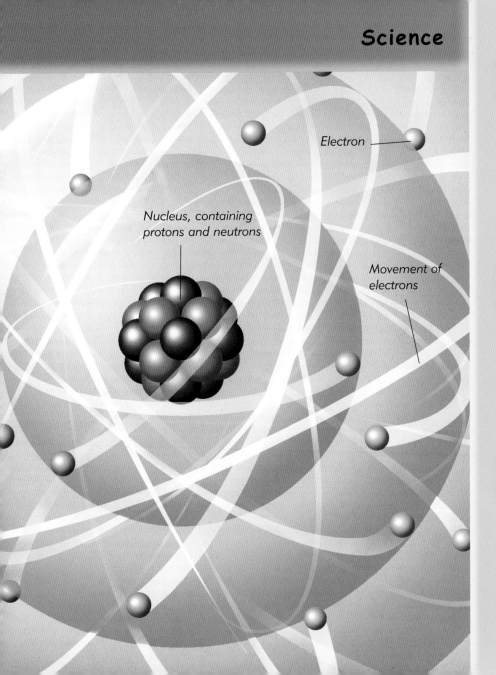

Science

Nucleus, containing protons and neutrons

Electron

Movement of electrons

Proton

Electron

Hydrogen is a gas with just one proton.

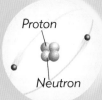

Proton

Neutron

Helium is a gas with two protons and two neutrons.

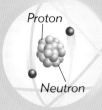

Proton

Neutron

Oxygen, the gas we need to breathe, has eight protons and eight neutrons.

133

Science and nature

Science and its effects are found all over the natural world. Scientists study animals, plants, rocks and soil. They want to understand nature and find out how science and its technology affect wildlife. One of the most complicated types of science is ecology. Ecologists study how animals and plants live and grow.

▲ Scientists study the damage and pollution power stations, factories and heavy traffic have on the environment. They then try to solve these problems.

Science

▼ Scientists study sharks around the world – especially how they live, behave and travel. A shark can be fitted with a radio tag, so scientists can record its movements.

Birds can be followed by radar, which is also used to detect planes.

Plants and their soil are studied by ecologists.

◄ Radio beacons can be used to track animals in the wild. Radio signals are sent out and picked up by satellites in space.

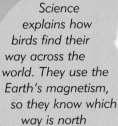

Fun fact!

Science explains how birds find their way across the world. They use the Earth's magnetism, so they know which way is north or south.

Healthy science

One of the largest areas of science is medicine.
Medical scientists work to produce better drugs,
more spare parts for the body and more machines
for hospitals. They also carry out
scientific research to find out
how people can stay healthy
and prevent disease.

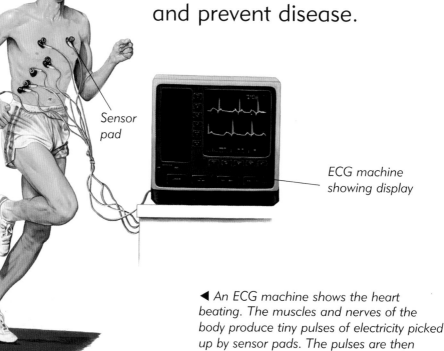

Sensor
pad

ECG machine
showing display

◄ An ECG machine shows the heart
beating. The muscles and nerves of the
body produce tiny pulses of electricity picked
up by sensor pads. The pulses are then
displayed as a wavy line on the screen.

Make a pulse machine

You will need:
modelling clay • a drinking straw

1. Find your pulse by feeling your wrist.

2. Place some modelling clay on this area, and stick a drinking straw into it. Watch the straw twitch with each heartbeat.

3. Now you can see and feel your pulse. Check your pulse rate by counting the number of heartbeats in one minute.

The heart pumps harder the more tired you become.

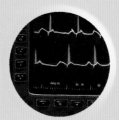

ECG machines test how healthy your heart is.

Laser surgery can be used to treat people who are short-sighted or long-sighted.

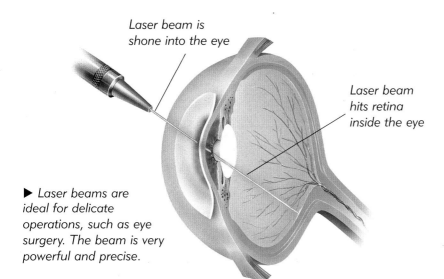

Laser beam is shone into the eye

Laser beam hits retina inside the eye

▶ Laser beams are ideal for delicate operations, such as eye surgery. The beam is very powerful and precise.

Dinosaurs

The dinosaurs first appeared on Earth
millions of years ago. Some were as small
as a pet cat, others were as big as a truck.
Discover what they looked like, how they
hunted for food, if they looked after their
young – and why they all died out.

The dinosaur world

Dinosaurs were reptiles – a group of animals with scaly skin that lived millions of years ago. There were many different kinds of dinosaur, but they all died out long, long ago.

▼ *There were many different types of dinosaur. Some walked on two legs and some walked on four legs. Some dinosaurs were carnivores (meat eaters) and some were herbivores (plant eaters).*

Key

1. Ornithosuchus
2. Eoraptor
3. Thecodontosaurus
4. Herrerasaurus
5. Saltopus
6. Scaphonyx
7. Procompsognathus
8. Mussaurus

Scaphonyx *was not a dinosaur, but a beaked reptile.*

Ornithosuchus *was part of the reptile group called thecodonts and was not a dinosaur.*

Saltopus *was a tiny dinosaur, about the size of a pet cat.*

When were they around?

Dinosaurs lived between 230 million and 65 million years ago. This vast length of time is called the Mesozoic Era, or the Age of Dinosaurs. The Mesozoic Era was split into three time periods – the Triassic, Jurassic and Cretaceous.

Dinosaurs

▼ The Jurassic Period was 203 million to 135 million years ago. Many new dinosaurs began to develop, such as the long-necked herbivore, Barosaurus.

Key

1. Cetiosaurus
2. Scelidosaurus
3. Dilophosaurus
4. Yunnanosaurus
5. Eustreptospondylus
6. Anchisaurus
7. Barosaurus
8. Heterodontosaurus
9. Shunosaurus

Barosaurus had a very long neck so it could reach the leaves on trees.

Dilophosaurus used its sharp, curved teeth to catch and eat its prey.

Fun fact!

The word dinosaur means 'terrible lizard'. However, dinosaurs weren't really lizards, and not all of them were terrible!

Life before dinosaurs

Dinosaurs were not the first animals on Earth.
Many other creatures lived before them, including other types of reptiles. Over millions of years, one of these groups of reptiles changed very slowly, or evolved, into the first dinosaurs.

▲ Dimetrodon was a fierce reptile that looked like a dinosaur – but it wasn't. It lived 270 million years ago, before the time of the dinosaurs.

Dinosaurs

Erythrosuchus was an early crocodile that lived before the first dinosaurs.

▼ Ornithosuchus was a small carnivore (meat eater) that walked on two legs. It was a cousin of the first dinosaurs.

Therapsids were reptiles with furry skin, like mammals.

Quiz time!

1. What type of animal was a dinosaur?
2. What is the name of the era in which dinosaurs lived?
3. What is a carnivore?
4. Which period is missing – Triassic, Cretaceous and?

Answers: 1. Reptile **2.** Mesozoic Era **3.** Meat eater **4.** Jurassic

Plants such as tree ferns grew during the Age of Dinosaurs.

The dinosaurs arrive

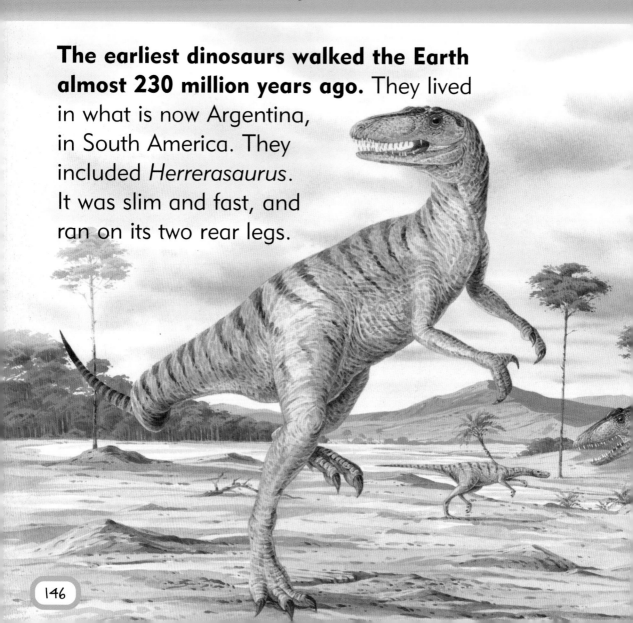

The earliest dinosaurs walked the Earth almost 230 million years ago. They lived in what is now Argentina, in South America. They included *Herrerasaurus*. It was slim and fast, and ran on its two rear legs.

Herrerasaurus *had legs directly under its body, unlike other reptiles.*

Make a dinosaur move!

You will need:

pencil • paints • stiff card • scissors • sticky tape • split pins

1. Draw a dinosaur without legs. Paint it any colour you wish and cut it out.

2. Draw two legs on another piece of card. Paint them and cut them out, too.

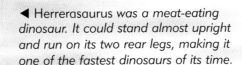

3. Fix the legs on either side of the hip area of the body using a split pin. Now make your dinosaur move!

The head was long, with a bendy neck to look for prey.

◀ Herrerasaurus was a meat-eating dinosaur. It could stand almost upright and run on its two rear legs, making it one of the fastest dinosaurs of its time.

The tail helped it to keep its balance.

Changing dinosaurs

As the early dinosaurs spread over the land, they began to change. This natural change in living things has happened since life began on Earth. New kinds of plants and animals appear, live for a time, and then die out as yet more new kinds appear. This is called evolution.

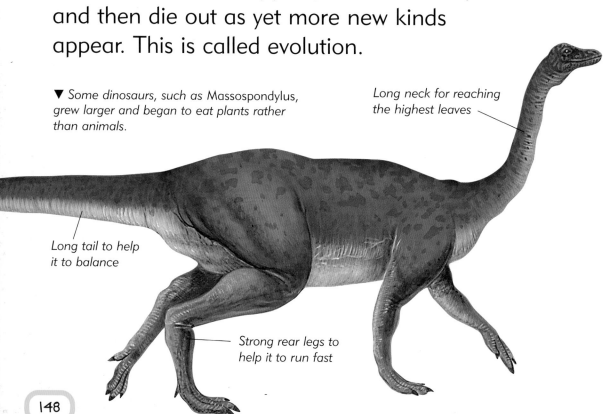

▼ Some dinosaurs, such as Massospondylus, grew larger and began to eat plants rather than animals.

Long neck for reaching the highest leaves

Long tail to help it to balance

Strong rear legs to help it to run fast

Dinosaurs

Riojasaurus weighed about one tonne – as much as a family car of today.

Plateosaurus was one of the first big plant-eating dinosaurs.

▶ Early plant-eating dinosaurs may have become larger so that they could reach up into the trees for food. Being bigger meant they were also safer from enemies.

Plateosaurus

Riojasaurus

▼ Rutiodon was a crocodile-like meat eater that hunted dinosaurs such as Plateosaurus and Riojasaurus.

Fun fact!

Early plant-eating dinosaurs did not eat fruits or grasses – these hadn't appeared yet! Instead they ate plants such as horsetails and ferns.

Gentle giants

The true giants of the Age of Dinosaurs were the sauropods. These enormous creatures all had small heads, long necks, long tails, barrel-shaped bodies and four legs.

▶ Barosaurus *was one of the biggest sauropods at about 25 metres long. Like most sauropods,* Barosaurus *had to eat for most of the day to get enough goodness for its enormous body.*

▼ *Some of the biggest sauropods were* Brachiosaurus, Argentinosaurus *and* Apatosaurus. *This scale shows how big they were compared to an adult human.*

Diplodocus *had peglike teeth for raking up leaves.*

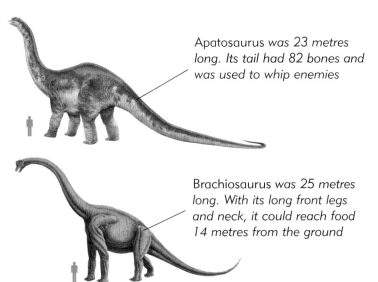

Apatosaurus *was 23 metres long. Its tail had 82 bones and was used to whip enemies*

Brachiosaurus *was 25 metres long. With its long front legs and neck, it could reach food 14 metres from the ground*

Sauropods *had flat claws that looked like toenails!*

▼ Argentinosaurus *was the biggest sauropod at 40 metres in length and 100 tonnes in weight.*

Fun fact!

Diplodocus *is also known as 'Old Whip-tail'! It could swish its long tail so hard and fast that it made an enormous CRACK like a whip.*

The biggest meat-eating dinosaurs were the largest predators (hunters) ever to have lived. Different types came and went during the Age of Dinosaurs. One of the last dinosaurs was also one of the largest hunters – *Tyrannosaurus*.

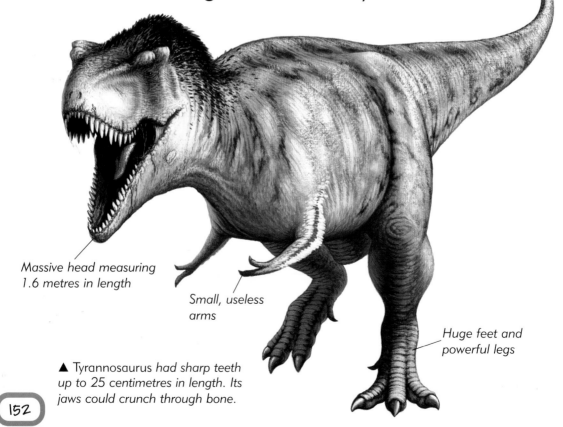

Massive head measuring
1.6 metres in length

Small, useless
arms

Huge feet and
powerful legs

▲ Tyrannosaurus *had sharp teeth up to 25 centimetres in length. Its jaws could crunch through bone.*

Eyebrow horns

Long tail

Powerful jaws
with long teeth

Sharp-clawed
hands

Long, strong legs
and clawed feet

▲ Allosaurus was a big, fast-moving
hunter with powerful jaws. It lived millions
of years before Tyrannosaurus.

Giganotosaurus
*is the biggest
meat-eating animal
that has ever lived.*

Spinosaurus *had a
'sail' of skin on its
back held up by
bony rods.*

Fun fact!

Some meat-eating
dinosaurs not only
bit their prey, but
also each other!
Fossils of several
Tyrannosaurus
had bite marks
on the head.

See, hear, smell

Like the reptiles of today, dinosaurs could see, hear and smell the world around them. We know this from the fossils of dead dinosaurs. Fossil skulls have spaces for eyes, ears and nostrils.

▶ Troodon *had very big eyes, which may have helped it to see in the dark when chasing prey, such as lizards.*

Make a Troodon mask

You will need:
card • paints • scissors • elastic band

1. Draw and paint the mask shown here.

2. Carefully cut out the mask and give it two large eye holes, like Troodon.

3. Make a small hole on either side of the mask to thread cotton through, so you can tie the mask onto your head and become a Troodon dinosaur!

Troodon's skull had large holes for the eye area.

Parasaurolophus may have used the tube-like crest on its head to make a noise like a trumpet.

Corythosaurus had a bony plate on its head, instead of a tube.

155

Slow or speedy?

Dinosaurs moved at different speeds, depending on their size and shape. Today, cheetahs and ostriches are slim animals with long legs that can run fast. Elephants and hippos are heavy and move slowly. Dinosaurs were similar – some were fast and some were slow.

◄ *Ornithomimus* could reach speeds of 80 kilometres an hour. That's faster than a horse at full gallop!

Struthiomimus *could run at 80 kilometres an hour.*

Coelophysis *could run quickly after its prey of lizards and insects.*

Quiz time!

1. What was the biggest sauropod?
2. How long were Tyrannosaurus' teeth?
3. Which dinosaur had huge eyes?
4. How fast could Ornithomimus run?

Answers: **1.** Argentinosaurus **2.** 25 centimetres **3.** Troodon **4.** 80 kilometres an hour

Muttaburrasaurus *could only run at 15 kilometres an hour.*

157

Eggs and nests

Like most reptiles today, dinosaurs produced young by laying eggs. These hatched out into baby dinosaurs that gradually grew into adults. Fossils have been found of eggs with dinosaurs still developing inside, as well as fossils of newly hatched baby dinosaurs.

▶ *A female Protoceratops scraped a bowl-shaped nest in the dry soil in which to lay her eggs.*

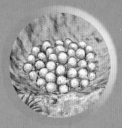

Protoceratops *laid its eggs in a circle inside the nest.*

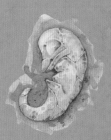

A fossilized baby *dinosaur developing inside an egg.*

Some dinosaur eggs *were leathery and bendy, like reptile eggs today.*

Design a dinosaur

You will need:
paper • paints

1. *Draw your own dinosaur – you could add horns, sharp teeth, sharp claws, a long tail, big eyes – anything you want!*

2. *No one knows what colour dinosaurs actually were, so you could paint your dinosaur any colour – purple and green with red spikes!*

3. *Name your dinosaur. You could name it after yourself, like Clarosaurus or Pauloceratops!*

159

Baby dinosaurs

Some dinosaurs may have looked after their babies, and even brought them food in the nest. Fossils of *Maiasaura* include nests, eggs, newly hatched young, and broken eggshells.

▼ Newly hatched Maiasaura babies stayed in their nest until their legs were strong enough for them to move around. The parents brought food, such as berries, to the nest for the babies to eat.

Baby Maiasaura were only 30 to 40 centimetres long.

The nest was a mound of mud. Up to 20 babies could live in it.

Fun fact!

Baby dinosaurs grew up to five times faster than human babies. Some were already one metre long when they hatched!

Dinosaurs in battle

Some dinosaurs had body defences, such as spikes, to protect them from predators. Most armoured dinosaurs were plant eaters. They had to defend themselves against meat eaters such as *Tyrannosaurus*.

▶ Ankylosaurus *could defend itself well. It had a large tail club to hit predators and its head and back were protected by large bony lumps and plates.*

Dinosaurs

Quiz time!

1. How long were baby Maiasaura?

2. Was Dimetrodon a dinosaur?

3. What is the biggest meat-eating animal ever to have lived?

Answers: 1. 30 to 40 centimetres
2. No, a reptile 3. Gigantosaurus

Ankylosaurus' tail club was one metre across and could deliver a painful blow.

Spinosaurus was a deadly carnivore with large, sharp teeth.

Ankylosaurus had spikes and lumps of bone on its back to protect itself.

163

Where did they go?

The dinosaurs died out 65 million years ago.
There are dinosaur fossils in rocks up to this
time, but none after this. However, there are
fossils of creatures such as fish and mammals.
Perhaps a giant rock (meteorite) from space
smashed into the Earth, killing the dinosaurs.

▼ *A meteorite would have thrown up clouds of ash and dust, blocking out the Sun. Plants would have died, leaving no food for the plant-eating dinosaurs. When they died too, the meat-eating dinosaurs would have starved.*

Volcanoes *could have erupted and choked the dinosaurs to death.*

Other animals *may have eaten all the dinosaur eggs.*

A giant tidal wave *may have drowned the dinosaurs.*

165

We know about dinosaurs mainly from their fossils. Fossils take millions of years to form. Most fossils form on the bottoms of rivers or seas, where sand and mud cover their bodies and begin to preserve (keep) them.

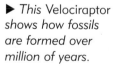

◄ *Velociraptor was a meat eater with sharp claws on each foot. It had powerful back legs to leap onto its prey to attack it.*

▶ *This Velociraptor shows how fossils are formed over million of years.*

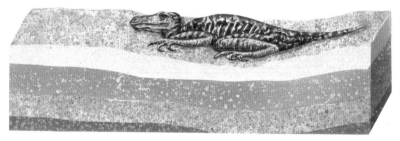

(1) *A dinosaur dies and falls into a river or lake. The soft body parts rot away, or are eaten by other animals.*

(2) The bones and teeth are buried under layers of mud. Tiny pieces of rock slowly 'soak' into the bones, filling any gaps.

(3) Over millions of year, these tiny pieces of rock replace the bones, but keep their shape. The bones have become fossils.

(4) If the rock containing the fossils is revealed, perhaps by wind or weather, scientists may find the fossils.

Tyrannosaurus *had deadly, sharp teeth.*

Dinosaur footprints *became buried in the ground and turned into fossils.*

Dinosaur skin *can sometimes form fossils and show how scaly it was.*

Finding fossils

Every year, thousands of dinosaur fossils are discovered. From the fossils, scientists try to work out what the dinosaur looked like and how it lived millions of years ago. Scientists who study prehistoric life are called palaeontologists.

Quiz time!

1. What big lump of rock from space could have destroyed the dinosaurs?

2. How long ago did the dinosaurs die out?

3. Where do most fossils form – on the land or in rivers and seas?

Answers: 1. Meteorite 2. 65 million years ago 3. Rivers and seas

Scientists dig into the rock with hammers and brushes.

Notes and sketches are records of what has been found.

Fossils are carefully lifted to stop them cracking.

169

Oceans

More than two-thirds of the Earth's surface
is covered by oceans. Discover life beneath
the waves – from tiny shrimps and colourful
fish to the mighty blue whale. Read about
amazing seabirds, deadly sharks and what
kind of creatures live in the deepest depths.

Sea mammals

Whales and dolphins are warm-blooded sea mammals. They need to come to the surface to breathe air. Sperm whales can hold their breath for up to two hours. This allows them to chase their prey, the giant squid. Dolphins can only hold their breath for a few minutes. They dive for fish and sometimes eat crabs and prawns.

▲ Bottlenose dolphins swim together around a group of fish. By working as a team, they can catch more fish to eat.

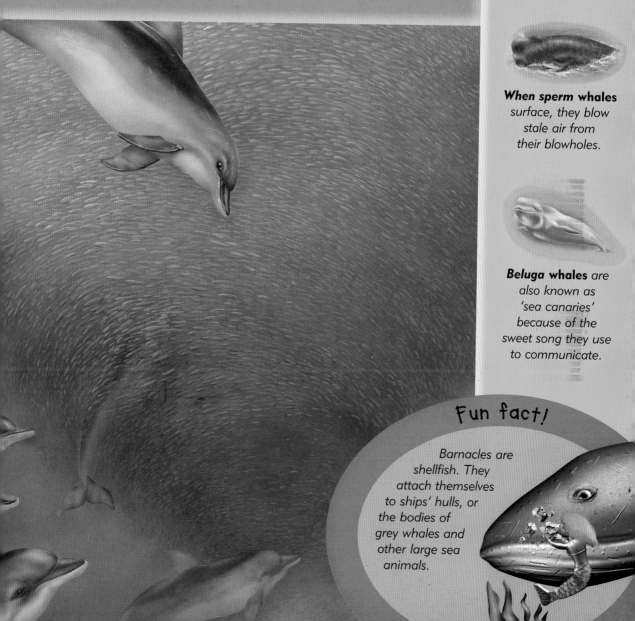

When sperm whales surface, they blow stale air from their blowholes.

Beluga whales are also known as 'sea canaries' because of the sweet song they use to communicate.

Fun fact!

Barnacles are shellfish. They attach themselves to ships' hulls, or the bodies of grey whales and other large sea animals.

Cold-blooded creatures

◀ When marine iguanas are not diving for food, they bask on the rocks around the coastline. The lizards' dark skin helps to absorb (take in) the Sun's heat.

Cold-blooded creatures, such as reptiles, cannot control their body temperature. This is why they prefer life on land, where it is easier for them to warm up. There are some reptiles that have adapted to ocean life, such as marine iguanas.

Marine iguanas live on the Galapagos Islands in the Pacific Ocean.

Banded sea snakes use venom (poison) to stun prey.

The venom of sea snakes is more poisonous than that of any land snake.

Mix and match

Can you match these sea turtles to their names?

1. Green
2. Hawksbill
3. Leatherback
4. Loggerhead

a.

b.

c.

d.

Answers:
1. c 2. b 3. d 4. a

▼ Banded sea snakes swim around coral reefs in search of their favourite food – eels.

◀ The yellow-bellied sea snake has a sneaky trick. Once its colourful underside has attracted a fish, it darts back – so the fish is next to its open mouth, ready to be eaten.

Deep-sea creatures

Few creatures can survive in the dark, icy-cold ocean depths. Food is so hard to find that creatures living there have very unusual features to help them survive, such as invisible teeth and their own fishing rods!

Cloud of hot water rich in minerals

▶ An amazing variety of life thrives in the deep sea near hot underwater vents.

Rocky chimney made from a build-up of minerals

Tube worms

Rat tail fish

Giant clams

◀ Black swallowers are just 25 centimetres long but can eat fish far bigger than themselves. Their loose jaws unhinge to fit over their prey and their body stretches to take in their huge meal.

Cookie-cutter sharks have large mouths and big, sharp teeth.

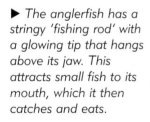

▶ The anglerfish has a stringy 'fishing rod' with a glowing tip that hangs above its jaw. This attracts small fish to its mouth, which it then catches and eats.

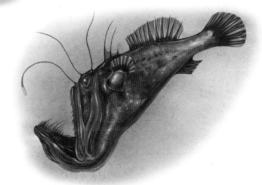

Dragon fish have light organs along their body to tempt prey and confuse hunters.

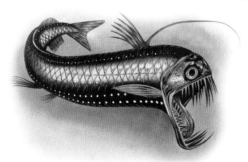

◀ A viperfish's long, snake-like fangs are invisible in the dark. Its prey does not realize it has entered the viperfish's mouth until it is too late.

Lantern fish have bodies that glow brightly in the dim sea water.

177

Super swimmers

There are over 21,000 different types of fish in the sea. Almost all are covered in scales and use fins and a muscular tail to power themselves through the water. They have slits called gills that take oxygen from the water so that they can breathe.

Fun fact!

Flying fish can use their winglike fins to keep them in the air for as long as 30 seconds!

▲ In a large group called a school, fish like these yellow snappers have less chance of being caught by hunters.

Oarfish grow up to 8 metres long. Their length helps to protect them from hunters.

Sunfish are so-called because they seem to sunbathe at the ocean surface.

The shape and colour of flounders help to camouflage them on the seabed.

Awesome jaws

Sharks don't have bones. Their skeletons are made of a gristly substance called cartilage. All sharks are meat eaters. Some filter tiny prey from the water, or lie in wait for victims on the seabed. Others speed through the ocean after prey.

▶ Great white sharks can speed through the water at 30 kilometres an hour.

Basking sharks eat huge amounts of tiny sea creatures called plankton.

▼ The blue shark is the most common shark, and is found in almost every part of the ocean.

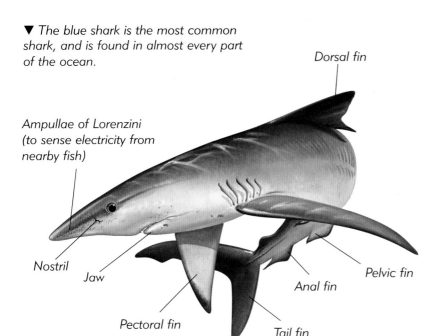

Dorsal fin

Ampullae of Lorenzini (to sense electricity from nearby fish)

Nostril

Jaw

Pectoral fin

Anal fin

Pelvic fin

Tail fin

Hammerhead sharks have a nostril and an eye on each end of their heads.

Quiz time!

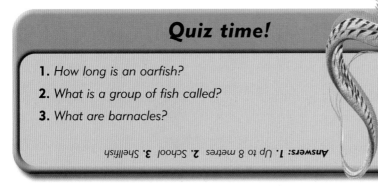

1. How long is an oarfish?

2. What is a group of fish called?

3. What are barnacles?

Answers: **1.** Up to 8 metres **2.** School **3.** Shellfish

Tiger sharks may produce as many as 40 babies at any one time.

Fast flippers

Seals, sea lions and walruses are warm-blooded mammals that have adapted to ocean life. These creatures are known as pinnipeds, meaning 'fin feet'. They have flippers instead of legs and a streamlined body. Instead of fur, they have a layer of fat called blubber to keep them warm in cold waters.

▶ *The male southern elephant seal is as big as a real elephant. It is almost 6 metres long and weighs about 5 tonnes.*

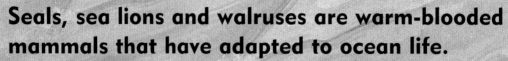

Sea otters live off the Pacific coast among huge forests of seaweed called kelp.

Walruses use their tusks to break breathing holes in the ice and to pull themselves out of the water.

Fun fact!

Leopard seals sing in their sleep! Found in the Antarctic, these seals chirp and whistle while they snooze.

Great travellers

Many ocean animals migrate (travel) incredible distances. Spiny lobsters spend the summer feeding off the coast of Florida in America, but head south in autumn to deeper waters. They travel about 50 kilometres along the seabed.

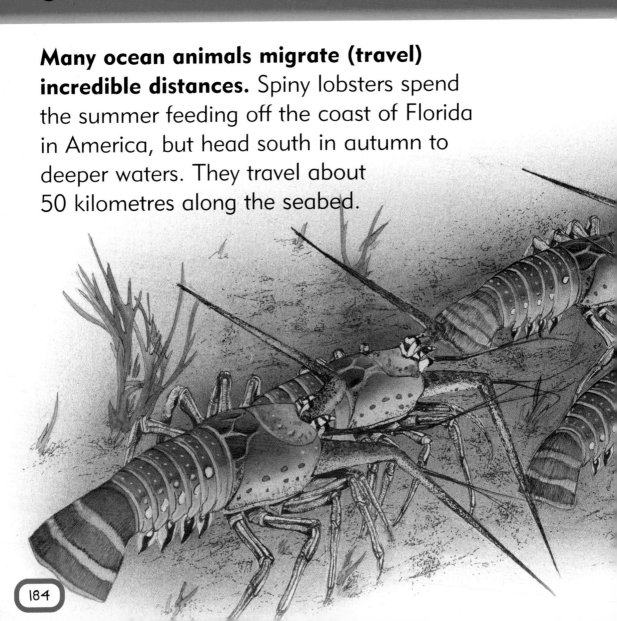

Oceans

Grey whales migrate 20,000 kilometres in a year – further than any other mammal.

Arctic terns can fly more than 40,000 kilometres in one year.

▲ Spiny lobsters travel in columns of up to 50. They keep together by touch, using their long, spiky antennae (feelers).

Fun fact!

Eels swim thousands of kilometres from the sea to lay eggs in the same place where they were born.

Air aces

▶ The wandering albatross is such an expert glider that it even sleeps whilst flying.

Wandering albatrosses are the biggest seabirds. With a wingspan of around 3 metres, these seabirds are so large that they take off by launching from a cliff. They mainly eat squid, but will also eat fish thrown from fishing boats. Many birds live near the ocean – birds with coloured bills, red pouches and colourful feet.

Gannets can dive into water from a height of 30 metres.

Identify the seabird

Match these seabirds to their correct names.

1. Grey-headed gull   **2.** Cormorant   **3.** Black tern

a.   b.   c.

Answers: 1. b 2. c 3. a

Male frigate birds puff up their red pouch to show off to females.

Boobies dance to show off their red or blue feet.

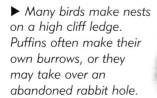

▶ Many birds make nests on a high cliff ledge. Puffins often make their own burrows, or they may take over an abandoned rabbit hole.

All kinds of penguin

There are 17 different types of penguin, mainly living in the Antarctic. They feed on fish, squid and krill. Their black-and-white plumage is important camouflage. From above, the black back blends in with the water. From underneath, the white belly is difficult to see against the sunlit surface of the sea.

Chinstrap penguin

Gentoo penguin

Adélie penguin

▼ *Penguins can swim, but not fly. They have oily, waterproof feathers and flipper-like wings. Instead of lightweight, hollow bones – like a flying bird's – some penguins have solid heavy bones. This helps them to stay underwater longer when diving for food.*

King penguin

Emperor penguin

Adélie penguins *build their nests from stones and small rocks.*

Emperor penguin *chicks are kept warm by nestling in their father's chest feathers.*

Fun fact!

The fastest swimming bird is the gentoo penguin. It has been known to swim at speeds of 27 kilometres an hour.

Mammals

This animal group has adapted to live in all kinds of habitats – from icy seas and frozen lands to steamy rainforests and scorching deserts. Discover how the cheetah catches its prey, why the biggest mammals live in the sea and which bat feeds on the blood of other animals.

What are mammals?

There are thousands of mammals living on Earth. Some can swim, some can fly and all are warm-blooded. Being warm-blooded means that mammals can keep their body temperature constant in any conditions, from hot sun to freezing snow. Many mammals live on land, but some, like the dusky dolphin, live in water.

▶ There are over 35 different kinds of dolphin. The dusky dolphin likes to swim near boats, and can leap and somersault above the waves.

Mammals

▶ Orang-utans are the largest mammals to live in trees. Like all mammals, the young orang-utan feeds on its mother's milk.

Pangolins are covered in hard scales for protection.

Red pandas sleep during the day and feed at night.

Beavers have flat tails and webbed feet, making them excellent swimmers.

Elephants on parade

You will need:
paper • pens • scissors

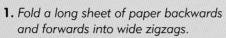

1. Fold a long sheet of paper backwards and forwards into wide zigzags.

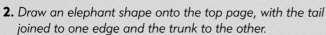

2. Draw an elephant shape onto the top page, with the tail joined to one edge and the trunk to the other.

3. Cut around the outline.

4. Draw ears and eyes onto each shape and colour them in. Open out your chain. All the elephants are holding trunks and tails!

Mammal families

Some mammals live alone, except for when they have young. Other mammals like to live in groups. Chimpanzees live in troops of between 15 and 80 animals. Dolphins can travel and feed in groups of up to 2000.

Mammals

▼ Zebras live in groups called herds. There are 5 to 15 animals in a herd – several mothers and their babies, and one male stallion.

Lions live in groups called prides. All other big cats live alone.

Koalas live alone in trees. They eat the leaves of eucalyptus plants.

Meerkats live in large groups called colonies of up to 30 animals.

Baby mammals

Most mammals give birth to their babies but some, such as the duck-billed platypus, lay eggs. All baby mammals drink their mother's milk. It contains all the goodness young mammals need to help them grow.

Mammals

Quiz time!

1. How many different types of dolphin are there?

2. Which animals live in a pride?

3. What is the biggest baby in the world?

4. Which animal has the longest pregnancy?

Answers: 1. 35 2. Lions 3. Blue whale 4. Elephant

Virginia opossums have more babies than any other mammal – as many as 21.

Elephants have the longest pregnancies of any mammal – about 20 months.

◄ The female puma, or mountain lion, gives birth to cubs (babies) with spotted fur. The spots disappear as the cubs grow older.

Blue whales have the world's biggest babies – measuring 7 metres in length.

Tallest and smallest

The blue whale is the biggest mammal in the world. It lives in the sea. It measures up to 33.5 metres in length – as long as seven family cars parked end to end. The elephant is the biggest land mammal, while the smallest mammal is the tiny hog-nosed bat.

▶ The blue whale is a true giant. It reaches up to 150 tonnes in weight – that's as heavy as 2000 adults or 35 elephants!

Mammals

Mouse deers are the smallest deers – they are as small as hares.

Capybaras are the largest rodents in the world.

Pygmy shrews have such small eyes, they rely on their senses of smell and hearing.

Mammal mix-up

You will need:
pens • paper • friends

1. *The first player draws the head of a mammal, giving it a long neck, then folds over the paper, so that only the neck shows, and passes it on.*

2. *Without looking under the fold, the next player adds a body to the neck, and folds the paper again.*

3. *The third player draws legs and feet and passes it to the last player. Unfold the paper. What a mix-up!*

Top racers

The cheetah can run faster than any other animal. It can reach speeds of 100 kilometres an hour, but it cannot run this fast for long. The cheetah hunts other fast-moving mammals, such as the brown hare or the pronghorn antelope.

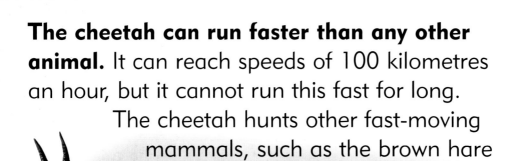

▼ The cheetah's long slender legs and muscular body help it to run fast when chasing its prey, such as the pronghorn.

Make a moving bear!

You will need:

pens • card • scissors • split pins

1. *Draw two circles onto card, for the head and body. Add ears to the head and cut the shapes out.*

2. *Draw a face onto the head and colour the bear in.*

3. *Draw four legs. Cut them out and colour them in, too.*

4. *Push split pins through the tops of the legs into the body of the bear. Now your bear can move!*

Pronghorns can only run at a speed of 70 kilometres an hour for a short time.

Brown hares have strong back legs to help them move quickly.

Red kangaroos can jump between 9 and 10 metres in a single bound.

High fliers

Bats are the only true flying mammals. They zoom through the air on wings made of skin. Flying lemurs don't really fly – they just glide from tree to tree. Other gliding mammals include flying squirrels and gliders.

◄ Flying lemurs can glide distances of up to 130 metres. They live in the tropical rainforests of Southeast Asia.

► Bats are small flying mammals that flit about at night after flying insects, such as butterflies. They grab their prey from the air while in flight.

◀ The American flying squirrel has a furry flap of skin along each side. When gliding, the squirrel steers by using its tail.

Fruit bats eat their own weight in fruit each day.

Vampire bats feed at night, usually on the blood of horses or cows.

Fun fact!

A vampire bat only feeds on the blood of other mammals. It drinks about 26 litres of blood each year!

Champion diggers

Many mammals live underground. They need sharp claws and strong front paws to dig through the soil. Badgers dig a network of chambers and tunnels called a sett. There are special areas in the sett for breeding, sleeping and storing food.

▼ *Badgers usually stay in the burrow during the day and come out at night. They line their sleeping areas with dry grass and leaves.*

Fun fact!

Badgers are playful animals – the adults are often seen enjoying a game of leapfrog with their cubs!

▼ *Sloth bears have long claws, which are excellent for digging up ants and termites. They then use their strong lips to suck up the bugs one by one.*

Moles *have special front feet for digging. They have poor eyesight but a good sense of touch.*

Volcano rabbits *dig burrows for shelter on the slopes of volcanoes.*

Ground squirrels *have strong front paws to help them dig underground.*

River mammals

Most river mammals spend only part of their time in water. Creatures such as the river otter and the water rat live on land and go into the water to find food. The hippopotamus, however, spends most of its day in water to keep cool.

▶ Webbed feet make the water rat a good swimmer. They help it to push its way through water.

▼ The water opossum is the only marsupial to live in water. It dives into the river to find fish.

Quiz time!

1. What is the biggest land mammal?
2. What type of mammal is a capybara?
3. Which mammal can run the fastest?
4. What do vampire bats feed on?

Answers: 1. Elephant 2. Rodent 3. Cheetah 4. Blood

▼ The duck-billed platypus uses its beak to find food in the mud of riverbeds.

River otters have short, thick fur to keep their skin dry.

Manatees are water-living mammals that feed on plants.

Hippos are not good swimmers. Instead, they walk on the riverbed.

207

Snow mammals

Mammals that live in very cold places, such as the Arctic and Antarctic, have thick fur to keep them warm. Also, the colour of their coats are very important. The polar bear, Arctic hare and snow leopard all have white fur to help them to hide in the snow.

Fun fact!

The polar bear needs its thick fur to keep out the Arctic cold – even the soles of its feet are furry!

▲ *The polar bear is the biggest land mammal in the Arctic. Its thick fur helps to keep it warm in the cold conditions.*

Male walruses
have long teeth
called tusks, for
digging up shellfish
from the seabed.

▶ The snow leopard lives in the mountains of central Asia. It has a grey coat, so that it is difficult to see in the snow.

Musk oxen have
long shaggy coats to
help them to survive
the Arctic cold.

▼ Harp seals are surrounded by snow, ice and freezing cold water. Their thick, white fur is waterproof so they can dive into the sea to catch fish.

Snowshoe hares
have brown coats
in summer, which
then turn white
in winter.

Fins and flippers

Most swimming mammals have flippers and fins instead of legs. Seals and sea lions have paddle-like flippers. They use them to drag themselves along on land, as well as for swimming. Whales and dolphins never come onto land. They swim by moving their tails up and down and using their front flippers to steer.

▶ Many kinds of dolphin live in groups called schools. They have smooth skin to help them slip easily through the water.

Whale of a time!

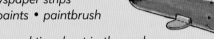

You will need:
long balloon • newspaper strips
papier-mâché paste • paints • paintbrush

1. Blow up a long balloon and tie a knot in the end.

2. Paste the newspaper strips onto the balloon. Repeat until the balloon has three layers of paper.

3. Leave it to dry for two days, then use a pin to pop the balloon.

4. Paint the whale blue and stick on paper fins and a tail.

Bowhead whales use filters in their mouths to catch food.

Narwhals have a long tooth growing out of their heads.

Killer whales are the largest members of the dolphin family.

In the rainforest

Rainforest mammals live at all levels of the forest, from the tallest trees to the forest floor. Bats fly over the tree tops and monkeys and apes swing from branch to branch. Lower down, smaller creatures, such as civets and pottos, hide among the thick greenery.

▼ Jaguars live in the rainforests of Central and South America. They are strong swimmers, and can often be found in swampy areas.

▶ *Dusky titis live in pairs in the Amazon rainforest. At dawn, they sit side by side on a branch, wrap their tails together and sing loudly.*

Tapirs live on the rainforest floor and have long, bendy snouts.

Civets live in the dense greenery of the rainforest floor.

▼ *The okapi uses its long tongue to pick leaves from forest trees. It lives in the African rainforest.*

Fun fact!

The sloth spends so much time upside down that its fur grows downwards – the opposite way to most mammals. This is so that rainwater drips off more easily.

Mammals that live in the desert have developed ways to escape the scorching heat. The North African gerbil, for example, burrows underground and only comes out at night. Not all deserts are hot, the Gobi Desert in Asia can be cold during winter.

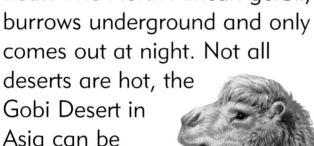

▶ The bactrian camel has thick fur to keep it warm during the cold winters in the Gobi Desert.

Kangaroo rats have strong back legs and can jump like kangaroos.

Quiz time!

1. What is the biggest land mammal in the Arctic?
2. Which mammal can walk on riverbeds?
3. What are the walrus' long teeth called?
4. Where do dusky titis live?

Answers: 1. Polar bear 2. Hippopotamus 3. Tusks 4. Amazon rainforest

▶ The North African gerbil is so used to desert life that it never needs to drink. It gets all the liquid it needs from its food.

Desert hedgehogs eat scorpions. They make sure to bite off the deadly sting first.

Fennec foxes have large ears to help them lose heat.

Plant eaters

Plant eaters spend much of their time eating in order to get enough nourishment (goodness from food). The good side to being a plant eater, though, is that the animal does not have to chase and fight for its food as hunters do.

▶ Nearly all of the panda's diet is bamboo. It eats fresh shoots in spring, mature leaves in summer and stems in winter.

Rabbits have strong teeth for eating leaves and bark.

▶ The giraffe's black tongue is almost 0.5 metres long. It uses it to grip leaves and pull them into its mouth.

Queensland blossom bats feed on flower pollen and nectar.

▼ Monkeys, such as the white-cheeked mangabey, mainly eat plants. They often live in tropical forests where there are plenty of fresh leaves and ripe fruit all year round.

Fun fact!

Some monkeys have a long tail that they use for climbing – like an extra arm or leg!

Hungry hunters

Mammals that hunt and kill other creatures are called carnivores. Lions, tigers, wolves and dogs are all carnivores. Many carnivores do not have to hunt every day – one kill will last them for several days.

▶ The tiger is an expert hunter. Creeping up on its prey, such as deer, it pounces and kills its victim quickly.

Cool cats!

You will need:
scissors • paper plate • paints • paintbrush
glue • paper • wool • elastic bands

1. Cut eye and nose holes in the plate.

2. Paint a cat face – maybe a tiger or a lion.

3. Stick on paper ears, and whiskers and a mane made from wool.

4. Make a hole at each side of the plate and loop elastic bands through the holes. Slip the bands over your ears and roar away!

▼ Bears are carnivores, but many eat more plants than meat. In summer, brown bears wade into rivers and catch fish with their mighty paws.

Hunting dogs hunt in packs, so that they can kill larger animals.

Wild boars are related to farmyard pigs. They eat plants and small animals.

Caracals can leap 3 metres into the air to catch a passing bird.

219

Birds

There are more than 9000 different kinds
of bird. Nearly all of them can fly, but some,
such as the penguin, cannot. Birds live all over
the world in every kind of habitat. Discover
the biggest bird of prey, read about the tiny
bee hummingbird – the smallest bird of all –
and find out which bird is the fastest flier.

Birds everywhere

A bird has two legs, a pair of wings and a body that is covered with feathers. Birds are, perhaps, the animals we see most often in the wild. They live all over the world – from icy Antarctica to the hottest deserts.

◄ All birds lay eggs. The egg protects the growing young. The parent birds, such as this song thrush, keep the eggs safe and warm.

Birds

▶ The wrybill lives in New Zealand, and is the only bird with a beak that curves to the right. It sweeps its beak over sand to pick up insects.

▼ Some birds attract mates by showing off their beautiful feathers. The male peacock has a long train of colourful feathers. When female birds come near, he spreads his tail, showing off the eyelike markings.

Greater flamingos use their beaks to filter food from shallow water.

Ostriches have strong legs so they can run fast.

Hornbills have hornlike growths on their beaks called casques.

The bird world

There are more than 9000 different types, or species, of bird. These have been organized by scientists into groups called orders. The largest order is the perching birds. These include common birds such as robins.

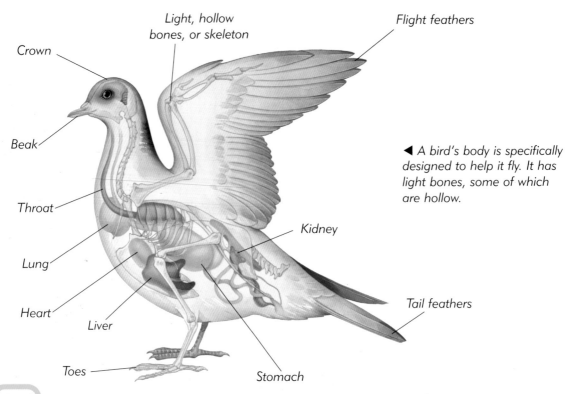

Crown

Light, hollow bones, or skeleton

Flight feathers

Beak

Throat

Lung

Heart

Liver

Toes

Kidney

Stomach

Tail feathers

◄ A bird's body is specifically designed to help it fly. It has light bones, some of which are hollow.

Birds

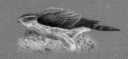

Goshawks are hunting birds, or birds of prey. They can kill animals as big as rabbits.

▲ Pigeons have strong wing muscles that help them to take off quickly and fly at speeds of up to 80 kilometres an hour.

▼ The robin can be recognized by its red chest feathers. The bright-red colour tells other birds to keep away.

Whistling swans are thought to have the most feathers of any bird – more than 25,000.

Fun fact!

Bird brains aren't stupid – ravens and pigeons can work out simple sums, while parrots can copy human speech!

Biggest and smallest

The largest bird in the world is the ostrich.
It is almost 3 metres tall and weighs up to
115 kilograms – twice as much as an
average adult human. The smallest bird is
the tiny bee hummingbird, which is only
about 5 centimetres long.

▶ Ostriches live in the
grasslands of Africa,
where they feed on
leaves, flowers
and seeds.

Bee hummingbirds are 5 centimetres long and weigh only 2 grams.

▶ Wandering albatrosses spend most of their time in the air. They have the longest wings of any bird – up to 3 metres from tip to tip.

Andean condors are the largest birds of prey at 110 centimetres long.

Roly-poly owl!

You will need:
scissors • empty yogurt pot • drinking straw
empty cotton reel • coloured paper • glue

1. Make two small holes at the top of the yogurt pot. Push a drinking straw through one of side of the pot, through the centre of the cotton reel and out through the other hole.

2. Cut out eyes, wings and a beak from coloured paper and stick them onto the pot. Now roll your owl around!

Collared falconets are the smallest birds of prey at only 19 centimetres long.

Starting life

A bird's egg protects the chick growing inside.
The yellow yolk provides the baby bird with food.
Layers of egg white cushion the chick. The hard
shell keeps the chick safe. The shell is porous –
it allows air in and out so the chick can breathe.
The parent birds take turns to sit on the egg to
keep it warm. This is called incubation.

▼ When it is ready to hatch,
the chick chips away at the
egg shell and breaks free.

③ The egg splits
wide open.

② The chick uses its
egg tooth to break
the shell.

① The chick starts
to crack the egg.

Birds

▲ Guillemots live on cliff tops. They do not build nests, but simply lay their eggs on the rock or bare earth.

Chicks have a small lump on their beaks called an egg tooth.

Emperor penguins only have one baby each year.

(4) The chick is able to wriggle free. Its parents will look after it for several weeks until it can care for itself.

Fun fact!

The guillemot's egg is pear-shaped, so that if the egg is pushed or knocked, it does not roll off the cliff.

Family life

Each species of bird has its own way of caring for its young. Emperor penguins lay eggs and rear (bring up) their young on the Antarctic ice. Hawks and falcons look after their young and bring them food for many weeks. Other birds, such as ducks and geese, are able to run around and find food as soon as they hatch.

Swans carry their young, called cygnets, on their back as they swim.

▲ Pigeons feed their young on 'pigeon milk'. This is a special liquid made in the lining of the bird's throat, called the crop.

Sparrowhawks are born blind and helpless, so need their parents' care for many weeks.

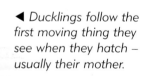

◄ Ducklings follow the first moving thing they see when they hatch – usually their mother.

Fun fact!

Penguins huddle together for warmth while they incubate their eggs. They take it in turns to stand on the outside of the group to take the force of the cold winds.

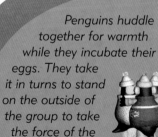

Bird homes

Birds make nests in which to lay their eggs and keep them safe. Nests can be made of twigs, leaves, mud or even saliva. They are built in a variety of places, such as trees, near water or in the walls of buildings.

▼ *The bald eagle makes one of the biggest nests of any bird. It is made of sticks and built in a tree or on rocks.*

Female hornbills lay eggs in tree holes. The males pass food through a small hole.

(1) The male weaver bird twists strips of leaves around a branch or twig.

◄ The male weaver bird makes a nest from grass and stems. He knots and weaves the pieces together to make a long nest, which hangs from the branch of a tree.

Cave swiftlets make nests from their own saliva.

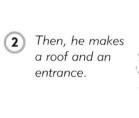

(2) Then, he makes a roof and an entrance.

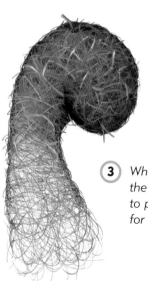

(3) When the nest is finished, the long entrance helps to provide a safe shelter for the eggs.

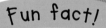

Fun fact!

Sometimes people collect the nests of cave swiftlets to make bird's nest soup!

Fast fliers

▲ *The peregrine falcon dives towards the ground to catch its prey, such as the swift.*

The fastest flying bird is the peregrine falcon.
It hunts other birds in the air and makes amazing high-speed dives to catch its prey. Ducks and geese are also fast fliers. The eider duck can reach speeds of more than 65 kilometres an hour.

Make a bird cake

You will need:
225 g of suet, lard or dripping • 500 g of seeds or nuts
empty yogurt pot • string • pan

1. Ask an adult for help. Melt the fat in a pan on a low heat and mix it with the seeds or nuts.

2. Pour the mixture into the yogurt pot and leave it to cool.

3. Remove the cake from the pot. Make a hole through the cake and put a string through the hole. Hang it from a tree outside and watch the birds eat the yummy treat!

Roadrunners can fly, but they prefer to walk or run.

Mergansers are ducks that can dive very quickly into the water to catch fish.

▶ Hummingbirds beat their wings more than 50 times a second as they hover in the air.

Swallows twist and zigzag in the air as they fly.

235

Swimmers and divers

Penguins are the best swimmers and divers in the bird world. They live in and around the Antarctic, an icy place at the very south of the world. They spend most of their lives in water, using their wings as strong flippers to help them swim.

▶ The gannet dives into the water, seizes it prey and surfaces a few seconds later.

▼ Emperor penguins can dive for more than 18 minutes.

236

Birds

Quiz time!

1. How many types of bird are there?
2. What is the horn-like growth on a hornbill's beak called?
3. Which bird has the longest wings?
4. What is another name for a hunting bird?

Answers: 1. More than 9000 **2.** Casque **3.** Wandering Albatross **4.** Bird of prey

Emperor penguins can dive deeper than 250 metres.

Northern gannets dive from great heights to catch fish from the sea.

Fun fact!

The gentoo penguin is one of the fastest swimming birds. It can swim faster than most people can run!

Night birds

Some birds hunt insects at night, when there is less competition for prey. These birds have special ways of finding their way in the dark. They might have a strong sense of smell or very sensitive eyesight.

▼ *The kakapo, from New Zealand, is the only parrot that is active at night.*

Birds

▼ Kiwis have a good sense of smell, which helps them to find food at night.

Poorwills hunt at night by opening their beaks wide to snap insects out of the air.

Barn owls have large, sensitive eyes to help them see in the dark.

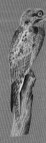

Oilbirds use clicking sounds to help them to find their way in the dark.

Feeding time

All birds have a beak for eating.
They have different kinds of beak,
suited to the types of food they
eat. Insect-eating birds, such
as antbirds, have thin, sharp
beaks for picking up tiny
prey. Hunting birds,
such as owls, have
hooked beaks for
tearing flesh.

▶ Fish owls eat more than
fish. They also grab lizards,
frogs, water rats, and even
young rabbits.

Birds

Toco toucans pick fruit and berries to eat with their long, strong bill.

◄ The antbird follows army ants as they march through the forest. The bird flies ahead of the ants and pounces on the insects and spiders that try to escape the marching ants.

► The Egyptian vulture steals other birds' eggs. It cracks the eggs by dropping them on the ground or by throwing stones at them.

Sparrows are happy to eat scraps of food put out on bird tables.

Marsh tits hide their food in the ground, or in cracks in tree bark.

Fierce hunters

Eagles, hawks and owls are all birds of prey.
These are birds that hunt other animals. The
golden eagle is one of the fiercest birds of prey.
When it spies a victim, it dives down and seizes
its prey in its powerful
claws, called talons.

Use your feet!

You will need:
different sized objects – pencils, books, coins

1. Get your friends together to see if you can pick things
up using your feet – like an eagle. Use anything you
want, such as pencils, coins, or even books!

2. Start with the easiest object, such as a pencil. Make
the objects harder and harder to pick up with your feet.
Whoever can pick up the most objects is the winner!

◀ *The golden eagle can soar for hours, searching for prey such as rabbits, birds and mice.*

Steller's sea eagles *swoop down and seize fish in their sharp claws.*

Ravens *mainly hunt rats and mice, but they can catch larger animals, such as rabbits.*

Crested serpent eagles *mainly feed on snakes and lizards.*

The rainforests of the world are home to a huge variety of bird life. One-fifth of all the birds in the world live in the Amazon rainforest, in South America. Birds of paradise are very colourful. They live in the rainforests of Australia and New Guinea.

▶ The blue bird of paradise is a very rare and can only be found in New Guinea and northeastern Australia.

◀ The scarlet macaw is named after its bright-red feathers. It lives in the tropical forests of South America, feeding on fruits and seeds.

Birds

Quetzals have tail feathers that grow up to 90 centimetres long.

◀ Found in the South American rainforests, the hyacinth macaw has a very powerful beak to crack open hard nuts and seeds.

Congo peafowls live in the thick rainforests of West Africa.

Quiz time!

1. What are the claws of a bird of prey called?

2. Which parrot is active at night?

3. What does a toucan eat?

4. Which bird is the junglefowl related to?

Answers: **1.** Talons **2.** Kakapo **3.** Fruits and berries **4.** Farmyard chicken

Junglefowls are related to the farmyard chicken.

Snow birds

The coldest places on Earth are the Arctic and the Antarctic. Here it is too cold for most birds to live all year round. During the Arctic summer, birds nest and feed on ice-free land called the tundra. In the Antarctic, most of the land is always covered in ice.

▶ Penguins live in the Antarctic. They have a thick layer of fat under their skin to protect them from the cold.

246

Handy penguins

You will need:
black sock • cotton • glue • white cloth
buttons • card • scissors

1. Glue the piece of white cloth to the black sock to make its chest feathers.

2. Make a beak out of card and attach it to the sock with some cotton. Stick on button eyes.

3. Cut holes in either side and push your hand into the sock, using your fingers as flippers.

▶ The snowy owl is the biggest hunting bird of the Arctic region. Snowy owls make their nests on the ground, amongst stones and moss.

The ptarmigan has white feathers to help it hide from enemies.

The snow bunting lives and breeds on islands around the Antarctic.

The tundra swan brings up its young on the Arctic tundra.

247

River life

Rivers, lakes and marshes are a favourite habitat, or home, for birds. There are plenty of fish, insects and plants to eat and places to nest. Herons, ducks and geese are commonly found in watery places, as well as kingfishers and pelicans.

◄ *Dippers live around fast-flowing streams and can swim and dive well.*

▶ *The kingfisher perches on a branch along streams and riverbanks, watching for any signs of movement of fish in the water. Then it swoops down to catch its prey.*

▼ Jacanas have long toes that allow them to walk on floating lily pads on the water.

Pelicans collect fish in the big pouch that hangs beneath their long beaks.

Herons stand in shallow water and grab their prey with their sharp beaks.

Ospreys are found near rivers and lakes. They feed mainly on fish.

249

Bugs

There are more insects, bugs and creepy-crawlies than any other animals on Earth. Most of these creatures are small, such as earwigs, ants and bees. Some are much larger, like bird-eating spiders and some kinds of scorpion. Read on to discover how bugs live, feed and rear their young.

Creepy-crawlies

Insects form the largest of all animal groups, with millions of different kinds, or species. But not all creepy-crawlies are insects. Spiders belong to a different group called arachnids and millipedes are in a group called myriapods.

▶ Honeybees live in nests where they make food from flower pollen and nectar. This food is honey.

Bugs

Cockchafer beetles can be found in woodland, farmland and gardens.

Tarantula hawk wasps only eat tarantula spiders.

Crickets are only active at night. They eat crops and plants.

253

Insects everywhere!

Insects, such as the housefly, are among the most widespread of all animals. There are many other members of the fly group, such as bluebottles, horseflies, craneflies and fruitflies. Other common insects include ladybirds, butterflies, ants and earwigs.

▶ *Craneflies have long, thin legs that are about twice as long as their bodies.*

Scorpionflies have a harmless sting on a long, curved tail.

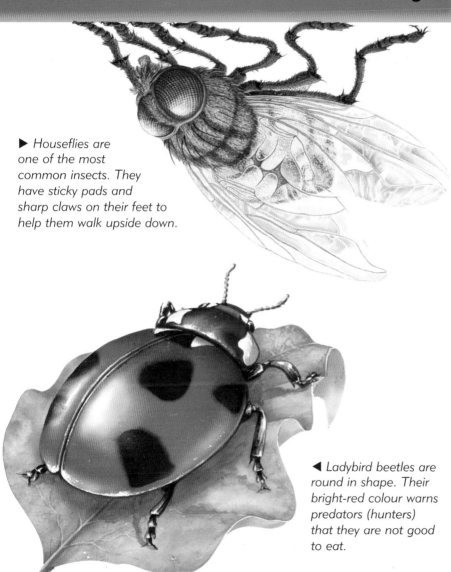

▶ Houseflies are one of the most common insects. They have sticky pads and sharp claws on their feet to help them walk upside down.

Ants make their nests out of leaves and mud.

◀ Ladybird beetles are round in shape. Their bright-red colour warns predators (hunters) that they are not good to eat.

Earwigs live in dark, damp corners – not ears or wigs!

255

Is it an insect?

Are all creepy-crawlies truly insects? One way to tell is to count the legs. If a creature has six legs, it is an insect. If it has fewer or more, it is another kind of animal. However, the young (larvae) of some insects, such as fly maggots, have no legs at all. But they develop into flies, which are insects.

▶ Pill millipedes have about 17 pairs of legs. They curl up into a tiny ball to protect themselves from predators.

Make a wormery

You will need:
see-through container • sand
soil • worms • leaves

1. *In a see-through container, put a 5-centimetre layer of sand, then a 5-centimetre layer of soil. Alternate the sand and soil until your container is almost full, then add leaves to the top.*

2. *Add some worms from your garden to the container, and keep it in a cool, dark place*

3. *Every few days, see how the worms mix up the layers. Carefully put the worms back where you found them when you've finished.*

▼ *Ticks are only the size of a grain of rice. They have eight legs, and are arachnids, not insects. They feed on the blood of other animals.*

Snails have hard shells to protect their bodies. They are molluscs, not insects.

Mites belong to the arachnid group, as they have eight legs.

Centipedes have 14 to 177 pairs of legs and belong to the myriapod group.

257

Insect homes

Some insects live together in huge groups called colonies, which are like insect cities. There are four main types of insects that form colonies – termites, bees, wasps and ants. An ant colony has one queen ant, and lots of female workers and male ants.

▼ Leafcutter ants cut bits of leaves from plants and carry them back to their underground nest.

▶ Some wasps build nests of paper, made from chewed-up bits of plants and wood.

Termites make their nests inside huge piles of mud and earth called termite mounds.

Cave crickets like to live in caves and other dark and damp places.

Ant-lion larvae live in sand or soil, waiting for their prey to pass.

Quiz time!

1. How many legs does an insect have?
2. Is a snail an insect?
3. When are crickets mainly active?
4. What do some wasps make their nests out of?

Answers: 1. Six 2. No, a mollusc 3. At night 4. Paper

Flapping around

Many insects have two pairs of wings. An insect's wings are attached to the middle part of its body, called the thorax. A large butterfly flaps its wings once or twice each second. Some tiny flies beat their wings 1000 times each second.

▲ The dragonfly is a fast and fierce flying hunter. It catches mosquitoes, flies and other small insects.

▶ The death's head hawk-moth has a skull pattern on its body. This is to warn predators to stay away.

Apollo butterflies are strong fliers. They can fly to the top of mountains.

Fireflies flash bright lights as they fly to help attract mates.

Mosquitoes are small flies with scaly wings.

Make a flapping fly!

You will need:
stiff card • tissue paper • scissors • sticky tape

1. Ask an adult for help. Carefully cut out the card to make a box with two open ends, as shown.

2. Attach strips of stiff card to the sides to make struts for the wings. Make the rest of the wings from tissue paper.

3. Hold the box as shown. Move the top and bottom walls in, then out. This bends the side walls and makes the wings flap, just like a real insect.

Hop, skip and jump

Many insects move around by hopping and jumping, rather than flying. They have long, strong legs and can leap great distances. This helps them to escape from enemies.

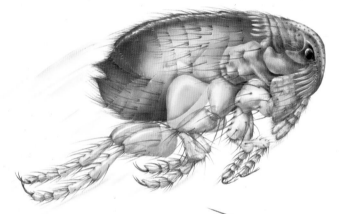

◀ Fleas are very tiny insects, but they can jump over 30 centimetres in length.

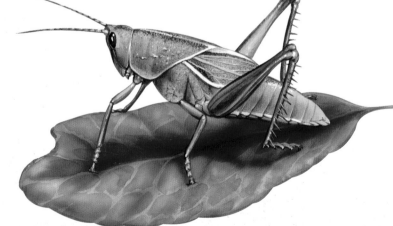

▶ Grasshoppers have very long back legs. Some types can jump more than 3 metres.

Quiz time!

1. Which flying insect had scaly wings?
2. Which insect can jump more than 3 metres?
3. Which part of their body do springtails use to jump?
4. Are mites insects?

Answers: 1. Mosquito 2. Grasshopper 3. Tail 4. No, arachnids

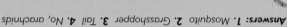

▼ Leafhoppers are strong fliers, but they can also jump great distances.

Click beetles can flick themselves 25 centimetres into the air.

Springtails jump with their tails, not their legs.

Crickets are all born with wings, but some can only hop from place to place.

263

Speedy bugs

Some insects hardly ever fly or leap. They prefer to run, and run, and run all day long, and even all night, too. Among the champion insect runners are cockroaches. Most scurry speedily across the ground on long legs.

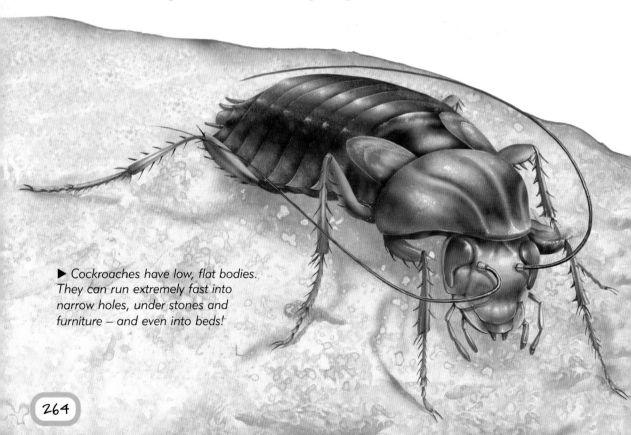

▶ Cockroaches have low, flat bodies. They can run extremely fast into narrow holes, under stones and furniture – and even into beds!

▼ The devil's coach-horse is a type of beetle that walks long distances to find food.

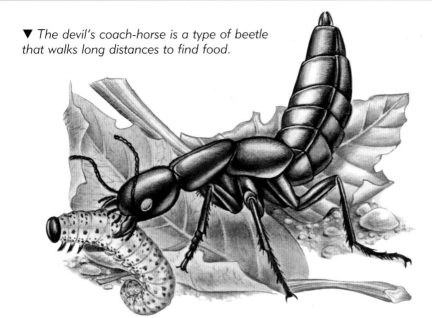

Oriental cockroaches are found in damp places such as drains and kitchen sinks.

Hissing cockroaches are named after the loud hissing sound they make when they breathe.

◄ Stonefly nymphs run around on riverbeds searching for food.

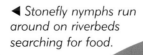

Fun fact!

For its size, a green tiger beetle runs ten times as fast as a person! It runs about 60 to 70 centimetres a second. That is like a human sprinter running 100 metres in one second!

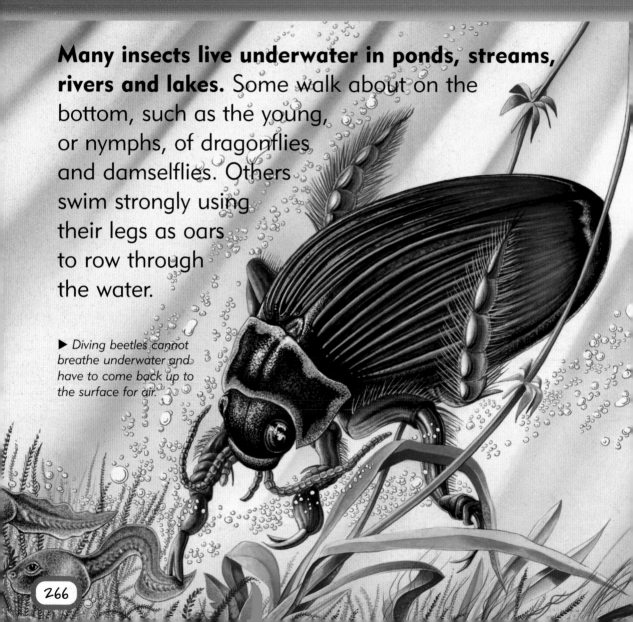

Swimmers and skaters

Many insects live underwater in ponds, streams, rivers and lakes. Some walk about on the bottom, such as the young, or nymphs, of dragonflies and damselflies. Others swim strongly using their legs as oars to row through the water.

▶ Diving beetles cannot breathe underwater and have to come back up to the surface for air.

Mayfly nymphs have tails with feathery gills for breathing underwater.

Pondskaters are slim and light so they can walk on water.

Great diving beetles hunt tadpoles and baby fish.

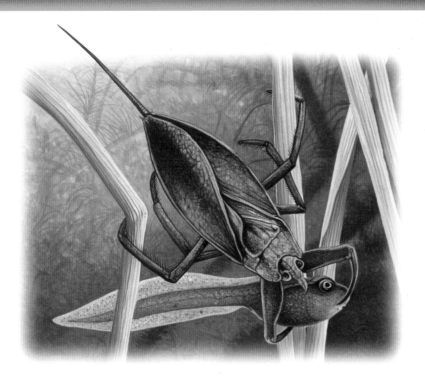

▲ Water scorpions live at the water's edge. They keep still and wait to pounce on tadpoles and other small water animals.

◄ Water boatmen live in ponds, canals and ditches. They have strong legs, which help them move through the water.

Burrowing bugs

The soil is full of millions of creepy-crawlies. Some are the wormlike young forms of insects, called larvae or grubs. Others are fully grown insects, such as burrowing beetles, ants, termites and earwigs.

▼ Earwigs live in soil and dig deep tunnels to escape the cold weather.

◀ Diplurans bury themselves in the soil. They feed on rotting plants and tiny insects.

Cranefly larvae are also called leatherjackets after their tough, leathery bodies.

Cicada larvae may live underground for more than ten years.

Cranefly larvae stay underground, feeding on plant parts for up to five years.

Bugs 'n' beetles

You will need:
tissue paper • sticky tape • paints
paintbrush • pipe cleaners • glue

1. Screw up the tissue paper into a tight ball.

2. Wrap the ball with another piece of tissue paper and hold it together with sticky tape.

3. Paint on eyes and tape on pipe cleaner legs. For a ladybird, paint the body red with black spots. For a bee, paint the body yellow with black stripes.

Insects may be small, but they are among the fiercest hunters in the animal world. Many have mouthparts shaped like spears or saws, which they use for grabbing and tearing up their prey. Some have very powerful bites and poisonous stings.

◀ *The praying mantis is one of the most powerful insect hunters. Its front legs have sharp spines and snap together like scissors to grab its prey, such as caterpillars and moths.*

Bugs

Quiz time!

1. What kind of insect is the devil's coach-horse?

2. Which insect is the fastest runner?

3. How many times can a honeybee sting before it dies?

4. Which insect can walk on water?

Answers: **1.** Beetle **2.** Cockroach **3.** Once **4.** Pondskater

▼ Honeybees sting only once and die soon after. The jagged sting remains stuck in their victim's skin, which tears out the honeybee's insides.

Sting

Lacewing larvae have jaws, which suck body fluids out of their prey.

Bombardier beetles squirt out a horrible liquid that stings their enemies.

Hornets are large wasps with very painful stings.

271

Hide and seek

Many insects are coloured and patterned to blend in with their surroundings. This is called camouflage. This makes it hard for predators (hunters) to see or find them. Or, if the insects are predators, camouflage helps them to creep up on their prey.

◀ Leaf insects are leafy green in colour and are very hard to spot among leaves. They are also called 'walking leaves'.

▶ Stick insects are excellent at camouflaging themselves, especially when they keep still or sway with the wind.

Make a camouflage scene

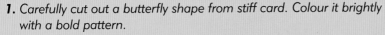

You will need:
card • glue • paints • scissors

1. Carefully cut out a butterfly shape from stiff card. Colour it brightly with a bold pattern.

2. Cut out leaf shapes from card. Colour them like your butterfly. Stick the leaves on a cardboard branch.

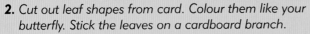

3. Your butterfly may seem far too bright to be camouflaged. Put the butterfly on your branch. See how well its camouflage works now!

▼ Many butterflies are brightly coloured. The brimstone butterfly looks like a leaf, which provides good camouflage.

Thornbugs have hard, pointed bodies. When they sit on twigs, they look like thorns.

Shieldbugs have broad, flat bodies that look like the leaves around them.

Bird-dropping caterpillars look like bird's droppings, so no animal would want to eat them!

273

Dinner time

About nine out of ten kinds of insect eat plants.
Many feed on soft, rich substances. These include
the sap (liquid) in stems and leaves, the nectar in
flowers and the soft flesh of fruits and berries.

▼ *Dung beetles roll animal droppings into big round balls.*
They roll the balls into their nests and feed on them.

▶ Termites feed on decaying wood, tree stumps and the roots of plants.

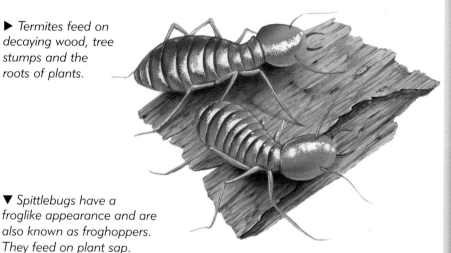

Furniture beetles like to eat the dead parts of trees and wood.

▼ Spittlebugs have a froglike appearance and are also known as froghoppers. They feed on plant sap.

Death's head hawk-moth caterpillars feed on potato plants and tomato leaves.

Fun fact!

Animal droppings are delicious to many kinds of insect. Some beetles lay their eggs in droppings, then the larvae hatch out and eat the dung!

What is a spider?

A spider has eight legs, so it is not an insect.
It is a type of animal called an arachnid. All
spiders are deadly hunters. They have large
fangs, which they use to grab and inject poison
into their prey, killing them. Like spiders, mites,
scorpions and ticks also have eight legs and are
part of the arachnid group.

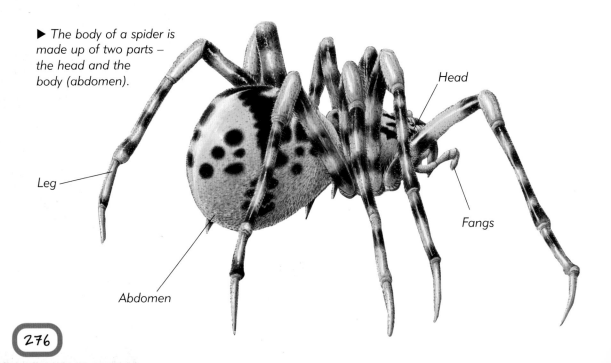

▶ The body of a spider is
made up of two parts –
the head and the
body (abdomen).

Head

Leg

Fangs

Abdomen

Make a spider's web

You will need:
card • scissors • cotton • PVA glue

1. *Ask an adult for help. Cut a large hole out of the middle of the card. Stretch a piece of cotton from one edge of the circle to the other, and glue or tape both ends.*

2. *Do the same again several times at different angles. Make sure all the threads cross at the centre of the hole.*

3. *Starting at the centre, glue a long piece of thread to each of the threads. Work your way round in a spiral until you reach the edge. That's the way that real spiders make webs!*

▶ The Australian redback spider belongs to the most deadly group of spiders called widow spiders.

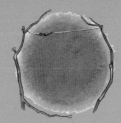

Stage 1
A spider starts a web by building a bridge.

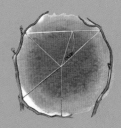

Stage 2
More threads are added to make a strong framework.

Stage 3
The spider fills the frame with circular threads.

277

The spider world

Not all spiders catch their prey using webs.
Some, such as the wolf spider, run fast and chase tiny prey such as beetles and slugs. Others, such as the trapdoor spider, hide themselves until an animal passes, then jump out to grab their victim.

▼ *The spitting spider has silk glands, which are connected to poison fangs. When it spots its prey, it spits a sticky silk over the prey to catch it.*

▶ Black widow spiders live in warm countries like the United States, Italy and South Africa. They kill their prey by wrapping them in thread and injecting them with their venom.

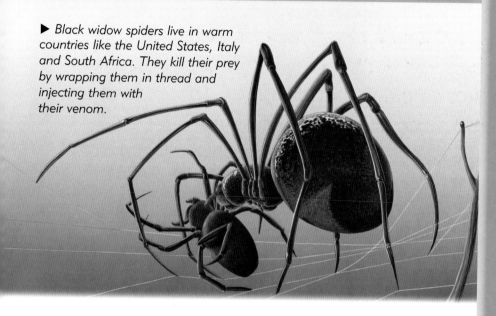

Crab spiders can change colour to blend in with their surroundings. This helps them hide from hunters.

Wolf spiders do not spin webs, they lie in wait and pounce on their victims.

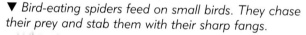

▼ Bird-eating spiders feed on small birds. They chase their prey and stab them with their sharp fangs.

Fun fact!

Tarantulas are huge spiders from South America and Africa. Stretch your hand out and it still would not be as big as some of these giants!

A sting in the tail

Scorpions have eight legs and are arachnids, like spiders. They live in warm parts of the world, such as rainforests and deserts. Scorpions have crablike pincers to grab prey, and powerful jaws to chop it up.

▼ *Scorpions have a dangerous poison sting at the tip of their tail. They grab their prey with their pincers and inject poison into the insect, killing it.*

Quiz time!

1. How many legs does an arachnid have?
2. Which insect has a froglike appearance?
3. Where on a scorpion's body would you find its sting?
4. Which spider can kill a human with its bite?

Answers: 1. Eight 2. Spittlebug 3. Tail 4. Black widow spider

Sun-spiders are fierce hunters with poisonous bites.

False scorpions do not have a sting in their tails.

Black widow spiders are dangerous – their bite can kill people.

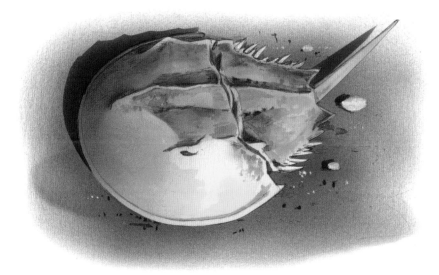

▲ The king crab has eight legs, so is an arachnid. It has a domed shell and spiky tail, but is harmless. It lives in the shallow waters off the coasts of North America and southeast Asia.

Ancient Egypt

Discover everything you need to know about ancient Egypt, including powerful pharaohs and magnificent monuments and tombs. Find out why the pyramids were built, how mummies were made and what kind of clothes the Egyptians wore.

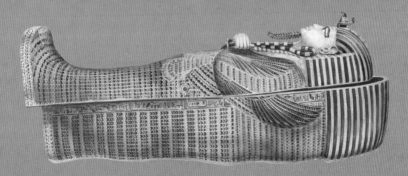

Life on the Nile

Without the waters of the river Nile, Egyptian civilization might never have existed. The Nile provided water for transport, drinking and watering crops. Every year, the Nile would flood, leaving a strip of rich, dark soil on either side of the river. Farmers used this fertile land to grow crops.

Ancient Egypt

▼ Most Egyptians lived on the banks of the river Nile, as this land was very fertile and they could grow crops.

Boats were the best way to get around in Egypt.

Papyrus reeds had many uses, including making boats and shoes.

Temples were built to worship the Egyptian gods.

Powerful pharaohs

The rulers of ancient Egypt were called pharaohs. The word 'pharaoh' means great house. The pharaoh was the most important and powerful person in the country. He owned all the land and ordinary people believed that he was a god.

Quiz time!

1. Who was crowned pharaoh in 1473 BC?

2. What is the name of the river that runs through Egypt?

3. How did Egyptians travel?

4. What does the word 'pharaoh' actually mean?

Answers: 1. Hatshepsut 2. River Nile 3. By boat 4. Great house

Ancient Egypt

◀ The pharaoh holds a hook and flail. They show his power in ruling the country.

Ramses II ruled for over 60 years. He was a great builder and a brave soldier.

Hatshepsut was crowned pharaoh in 1473 BC.

Fun fact!

Women courtiers sometimes wore hair cones made of scented animal fat. When the fat melted, it made their hair smell sweet, but look greasy!

Gods and goddesses

The ancient Egyptians worshipped more than 1000 different gods and goddesses. The most important god of all was Ra, the sun god. During the night Ra travelled through the underworld and was born again each morning. According to the ancient Egyptians, this was the reason the Sun rose each day.

◄ Ra the sun god was later combined with another god to become Amun-Ra. Amun-Ra became king of the gods.

Design a wall painting

You will need:

pens • card • paints

1. *Draw your own gods and goddesses – you can add crowns, wings, masks – anything you want!*

2. *Paint them lots of bright colours.*

3. *Hang the painting on your wall for your very own Egyptian wall painting!*

Horus *was the god of the sky. He had the head of a falcon.*

Osiris and Isis *were in charge of the underworld.*

▼ *Anubis was in charge of preparing bodies to be mummified. As jackals were often found near cemeteries, Anubis was given the head of a jackal.*

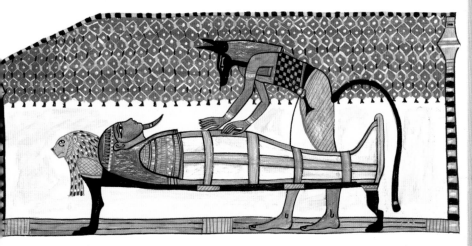

Anubis, *the jackal-headed god, watched over the dead.*

The great pyramids

The three pyramids at Giza are more than 4500 years old. They were built for three kings – Khufu, Khafre and Menkaure. After the kings died, their bodies were preserved as mummies and buried inside the pyramids. The Great Pyramid is the biggest pyramid in the world. It took more than 20 years to build.

Blocks of limestone were moved by wooden sledges

Ancient Egypt

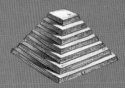

The Step Pyramid is one of the world's oldest pyramids.

The huge stones were levered into exactly the right position

Teams of workers pulled the stones up the slopes

The Great Sphinx at Giza is a stone statue that is half-lion, half-human. It guards the way to the Great Pyramid.

▲ The Great Pyramid was built with more than 2 million blocks of limestone. Each block weighed as much as two and a half adult elephants!

Fun fact!

A special guide for tomb robbers called The Book of Buried Pearls gave details of fabulous treasures hidden inside the pyramids!

Temples and tombs

The ancient Egyptians built magnificent buildings, including temples and tombs. From 2150 BC, pharaohs were not buried in pyramids, but in tombs in the Valley of the Kings. Gods, such as Amun-Ra were worshipped in temples.

▲ *The temple at Abu Simbel is carved out of sandstone rock. Four enormous statues of Ramses II guard the entrance. They are more than 20 metres high.*

Ancient Egypt

The death mask of Tutankhamun was found at the Valley of the Kings in 1922.

Ancient Egyptians decorated tomb and temple walls with paintings.

Fun fact!

Queen Hapshepsut wore the royal crown and the ceremonial beard when she became pharaoh!

▲ The Great Hall at Karnak was also built by Ramses II. It has 134 papyrus columns that are up to 21 metres tall.

Mummification

Making a mummy was skilled work.
The body's insides were removed, except for the heart. Next, the body was left to dry for 40 days. Then it was washed and filled with linen to keep its shape. Finally, the body was covered in oil and wrapped in linen bandages.

Wooden coffin for the body

Make a death mask

You will need:

play mask • PVA glue • paintbrush
newspaper • paints

1. Cover the mask in PVA glue.

2. Tear the newspaper into strips. Layer the strips over the mask and leave to dry.

3. Cover the mask with white paint. Leave to dry.

4. Use the paints to create your own death mask!

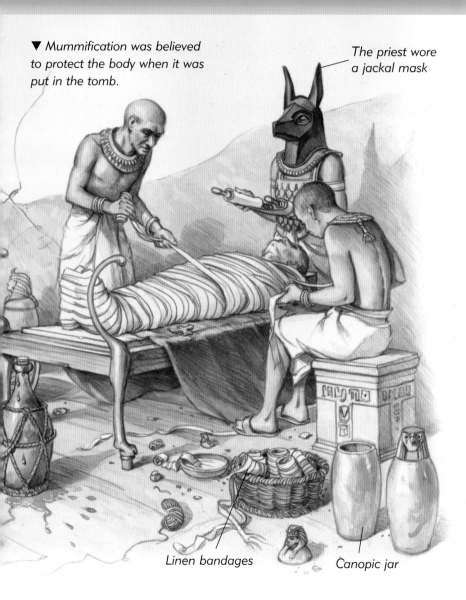

▼ Mummification was believed to protect the body when it was put in the tomb.

The priest wore a jackal mask

Linen bandages

Canopic jar

The priest wore a jackal mask to look like the god Anubis.

Canopic jars were used to store the dead person's body parts.

Wooden coffins were decorated with gold and jewels.

295

War and weapons

Egypt had a professional army of trained soldiers. The pharaoh was in charge of this army, and led his soldiers into battle. Egyptian soldiers used a variety of weapons including spears, daggers, axes and bows and arrows.

▼ *During the reign of Ramses III the Sea People attacked Egypt. Ramses sent a fleet of warships to defeat them.*

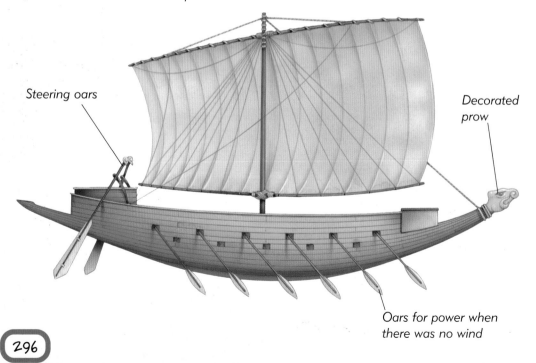

Steering oars

Decorated prow

Oars for power when there was no wind

Alexander the Great conquered Egypt and made himself pharaoh.

▲ Specially trained soldiers fired arrows from horse-drawn chariots. Each chariot carried two soldiers and was pulled by a pair of horses.

The bow and arrow was the most important weapon used in warfare.

▶ Foot soldiers carried a strong shield and a long spear.

Fun fact!

Soldiers who fought bravely in battle were awarded golden medals that looked like flies – for 'stinging' the enemy so successfully!

Buying and selling

Egyptian traders did not use money to buy and sell goods. Instead they exchanged goods with foreign traders. This was called bartering. Merchants visited nearby countries and offered things such as cattle, gold and a kind of paper called papyrus. In return they were given goods such as silver, cedar wood and ivory.

▶ An ancient Egyptian town had its own market place, where people went to buy food, pots, pans and other everyday goods.

Ancient Egypt

Egyptians took their goods to market to exchange for other items.

Market stalls sold all kinds of fruits and vegetables.

Fun fact!

Fly swatters made from giraffe tails were a popular fashion item in ancient Egypt.

Farming the land

The farming year was divided into three seasons – the flood, the growing period and the harvest.
After the floods, farmers prepared the soil and planted the seeds by hand. Then came the harvest, when the crops were gathered.

▼ Workers gathered the grain by throwing the grain and chaff (grain shell) into the air so that the heavier grain dropped to the floor.

Ancient Egypt

Fruits and vegetables grew well in the strips of rich, dark soil.

Quiz time!

1. Who was married to Osiris?
2. What did the Egyptians use as fly swatters?
3. Who was in charge of the army?

Answers: 1. Isis **2.** Giraffe tails **3.** Pharaoh

A shaduf was a device used for lifting water from the Nile.

▲ Tax collectors would often decide how rich people were by counting how many cattle they owned.

Fun fact!

Sometimes farmers hired flute players to keep people company while they worked.

The working life

Most people worked as craftworkers or farm labourers, including potters, carpenters, weavers, jewellers and shoemakers. Scribes were important people in ancient Egypt. Unlike ordinary Egyptians, scribes knew how to read and write. They kept records of daily events.

▶ Craftworkers had special areas within the town where they produced statues and furniture for the pharaoh.

Ancient Egypt

Quiz time!

Can you name the following items from ancient Egypt?

1.
2.
3.

Answers: 1. Tutankhamun's death mask **2.** Step Pyramid **3.** Great Sphinx

▶ Only the sons of scribes went to school to learn how to read and write. Then they could be scribes, too.

Workers often made a living by selling their goods at the market.

A typical lunch for a worker was bread and onions, washed down with beer.

Rich families had servants, who worked as maids, cooks and gardeners.

303

Life at home

Egyptian houses were made from mud bricks dried in the sun. The inside walls were covered with thick plaster, which helped keep the houses cool in the hot weather. Wealthy Egyptians lived in villas in the countryside. Poorer families lived mostly in a crowded single room.

▶ Family was the centre of ancient Egyptian life and many different generations of Egyptians shared a home together.

Quiz time!

1. What did Egyptians decorate tombs with?
2. Which part of the body was left inside a mummy?
3. What is the name of the device used for lifting water?
4. Who knew how to read and write?

Answers: 1. Paintings 2. Heart 3. Shaduf 4. Scribes

Ancient Egypt

Mud was shaped into bricks and left to dry in the Sun.

Oil lamps made of clay were used as lights.

The dwarf god, Bes, was the Egyptian god of the home.

Dressing up

In Egypt, both men and women wore eye make-up. The Egyptians believed that a special black eye paint, called kohl, had magical healing powers and could cure poor eyesight and fight eye infections.

▶ Egyptians liked to wear make-up. They decorated their eyes with kohl and eyeshadow. To keep clean, they also shaved their heads.

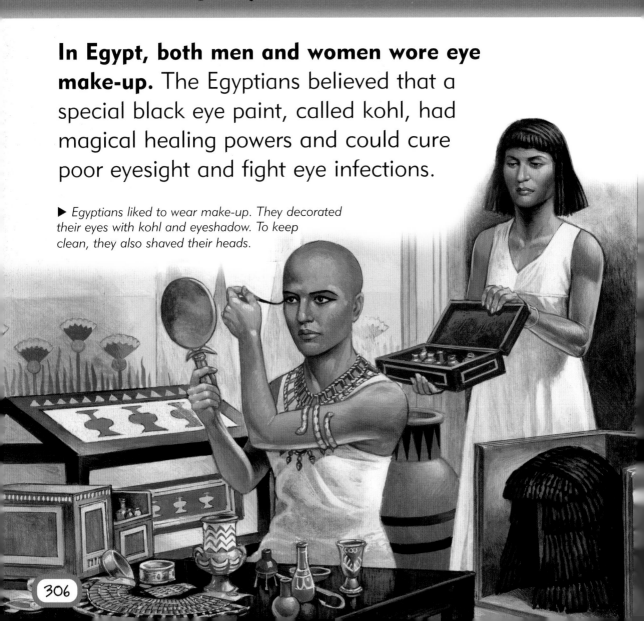

◄ Wealthy people wore wigs made from human hair or sheep's wool. They had to be stored on special stands in the home.

The eye of Horus was a good luck charm worn by Egyptians.

► Egyptians looked after their hair and wigs with combs made of wood and ivory. Sometimes, they even used curling tongs.

Clothes were made from linen to keep people cool in hot weather.

Make a magic eye charm

You will need:

clay • paints • paintbrush • varnish

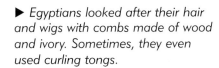

1. Shape the clay into the eye of Horus, shown here.

2. Leave the clay to harden.

3. Paint your charm with bright colours and leave it to dry. Varnish it to make it look extra shiny!

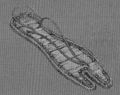

Sandals were made from papyrus and other reeds.

Travelling by boat

The main method of transport in ancient Egypt was by boat along the river Nile. The Nile is the world's longest river. It flows across the entire length of the desert lands of Egypt. The earliest boats were made from papyrus reeds. Gradually, wooden boats replaced them.

▲ Hippo hunting was a dangerous, but popular sport. Hunters in reed boats, armed with only spears and ropes, killed hippos in the waters of the river Nile.

Ancient Egypt

Large, rectangular sail

Lookout post

Cabin

Oar

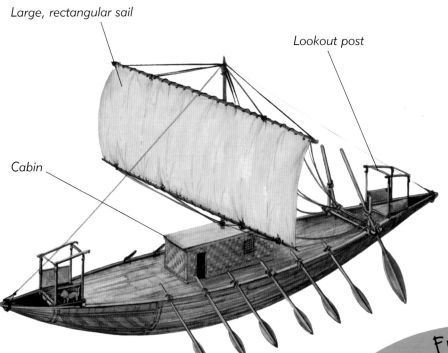

▲ Trading ships used both sail and oar power. They were kept close to the shore, and were fitted with a large rectangular sail and only a few oars.

Early boats were made from bundles of reeds tied together.

A carved boat was built to carry the body of King Khufu at his funeral.

Fun fact!

In 1970, a Norwegian explorer sailed a papyrus boat from North Africa to the Caribbean!

Painting words

The ancient Egyptians used a system of picture-writing called hieroglyphics. Each hieroglyph, or picture, represented an object or sound. The insides of many Egyptian tombs were decorated with hieroglyphs, often showing scenes from the dead person's life.

▼ *Several artists worked together to paint tombs with colourful symbols and scenes.*

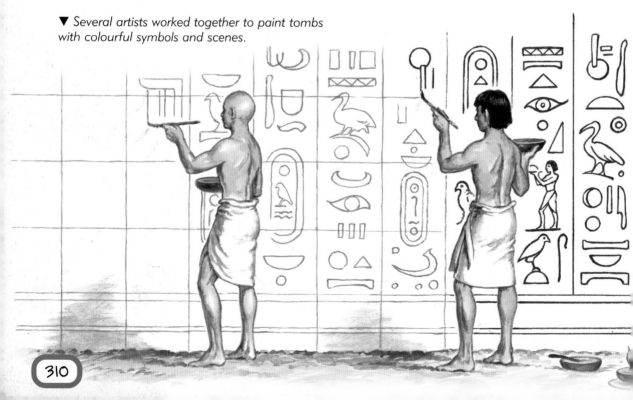

Write your name in hieroglyphics

Below is the hieroglyphic alphabet. You can use it to write your name or letters to your friends.

A	B	C	D	E	F	G	H	I	J	K	L	M

N	O	P	Q	R	S	T	U	V	W	X	Y	Z

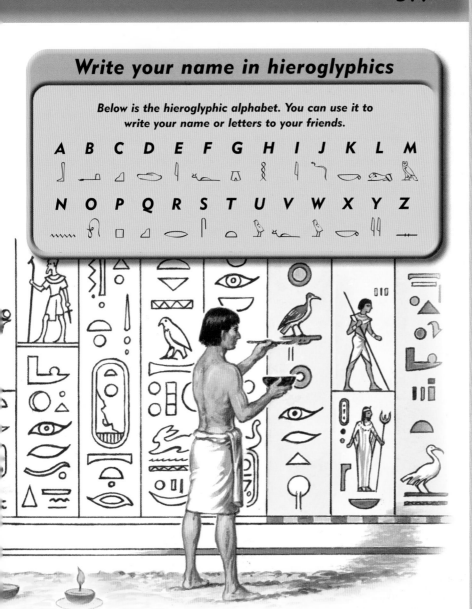

A junior artist drew the outlines of the scenes.

A senior artist checked and corrected the outlines.

A painter filled the outlines in colour.

Egyptian know-how

The ancient Egyptians had many skills. They not only invented their own alphabet, but they were the first to write on a kind of paper made from papyrus reeds. The Egyptians also used their knowledge of the stars to help build temples. Egyptian doctors understood the basic workings of the human body.

▶ Egyptian doctors knew how to set broken bones and treat illnesses.

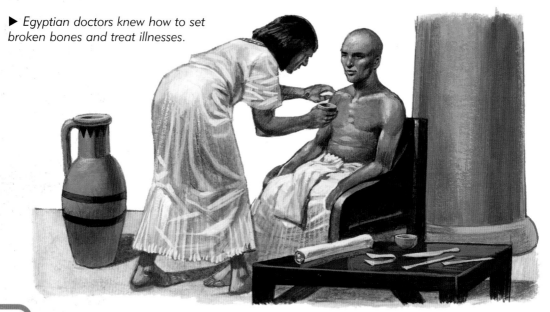

▼ *Papyrus was expensive because it took such a long time to make.*

(1)

Firstly, people had to cut down the papyrus stems, and cut them into lots of thin strips.

(2)

Then the strips were laid in rows on a frame to form layers.

(3)

The papyrus strips were then pressed under weights. This squeezed out the water and squashed the layers together.

(4)

Finally, when the papyrus was dry, the surface was rubbed with a stone to make it smooth for writing.

Papyrus scrolls were the first kind of paper ever used.

Ink was made by mixing water with charcoal or coloured minerals.

Reed brushes were used for writing on papyrus.

Ancient Rome

About 2000 years ago, ancient Rome was the most powerful city in the world. It ruled many other countries and was part of a large empire. Discover what Romans did for a living, find out how they built so many beautiful buildings, and visit the mighty Colosseum to learn about gladiator fights.

Rome and its empire

The city of Rome, in Italy, was once the centre of a great empire. An empire is made up of many different countries ruled by one person. The city began around 1000 BC as a village of huts, but soon became rich and powerful, ruling over 50 million people around the world.

Mosaic madness

You will need:
pencil • paper • glue
coloured paper squares

1. Draw the outline of your design – perhaps a fish – on a large sheet of paper.
2. Stick the coloured squares onto the large sheet of paper, following the outlines of your design, and create a Roman mosaic!

▶ The city of Rome was busy, noisy and exciting, with many beautiful buildings.

Ancient Rome

Soldiers march through Rome to celebrate a victory at war.

The emperor led the victory parade on a golden chariot.

Slaves captured during battle were tied up and walked through the city.

Building Rome

The Romans invented many new building materials and techniques. They were the first to make concrete, which was much cheaper and easier to use than solid building stone. They also discovered how to build arches to create tall, strong doorways. They even invented special pumps that pushed water uphill.

▶ The Romans were amazing builders and architects. Their roads and many of their buildings have lasted over 2000 years.

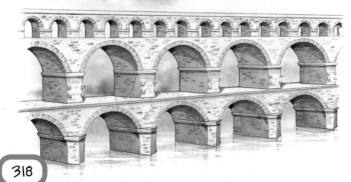

◀ Each day, aqueducts brought fresh water from the hills into Rome. This water was used in public fountains and the homes of rich people.

Ancient Rome

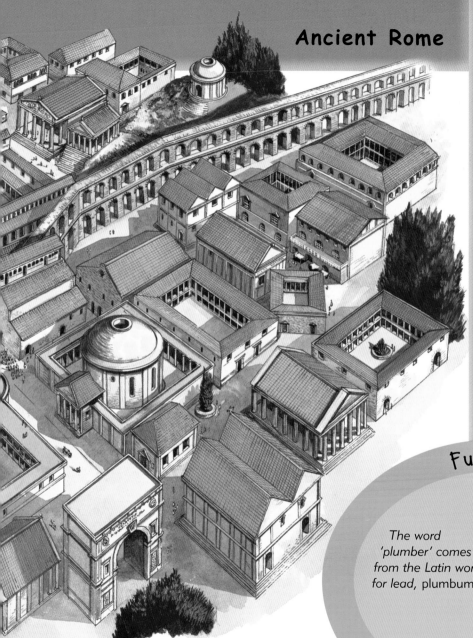

Domes were designed for the roofs of large buildings.

Arches were built in honour of the emperor.

Fun fact!

The word 'plumber' comes from the Latin word for lead, plumbum.

Rulers of Rome

Rome was once ruled by kings. According to legend, the first king was Romulus, who came to power in 753 BC. In 509 BC the last king, Tarquin the Proud, was overthrown. Rome then became a republic – a state without a king. After many years of civil war, an army general called Octavian took power, bringing peace and better laws to Rome. He took the name Augustus and became the first emperor of Rome.

▼ *According to legend, after being brought up by a wolf, Romulus and Remus were the founders of Rome. Romulus named the city after himself.*

▶ In 47 BC, a successful general called Julius Caesar declared himself dictator. His reign ended in 44 BC when he was killed.

Roman coins showed the most powerful people of the time, usually the emperor.

The republic of Rome was ruled by a group of people called the Senate.

▲ Octavian became the first emperor of Rome in 27 BC. During his reign, he ended civil war and introduced many new laws.

Fun fact!

The mad Emperor Nero was said to have laughed and played music while watching a terrible fire destroy part of Rome.

Gods and goddesses

The Romans worshipped many gods and goddesses. The Roman emperor offered sacrifices to the gods who protected Rome. Ordinary Roman people also made offerings of food, wine and incense to the gods.

▶ There was a god for almost everything, from love and war to wild animals and people's homes.

Gods and goddesses key

① Mars, god of war

② Venus, goddess of love

③ Jupiter, king of the gods

④ Juno, queen of the gods

⑤ Neptune, god of the sea

⑥ Minerva, goddess of war

⑦ Diana, goddess of the moon and hunting

⑧ Mercury, messenger of the gods

⑨ Pan, god of the mountainside, pastures, sheep and goats

People wrote messages to the gods asking them to curse their enemies.

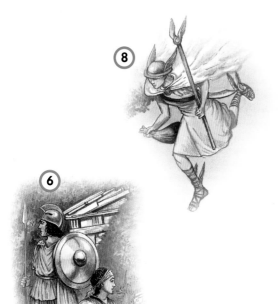

A family shrine was like a mini church inside people's homes.

Fun fact!

After an animal had been sacrificed to the gods, a priest examined its liver. If it was diseased, bad luck was on the way!

The people of Rome

By around AD 300, Rome was the largest city in the world. Over one million people lived there. The government was run by nobles and knights who were usually very rich. Ordinary citizens, called Plebeians, were poor but they could vote and serve in the army. Slaves could not leave their owners and had no rights.

◄ Slaves were bought and sold at slave-markets. They were paraded before the citizens to be chosen or rejected.

▼ The Forum was the heart of the city. It was a large marketplace, surrounded by government buildings.

City guards protected Rome from outside attackers.

Senators were important government leaders.

Fun fact!

Roman engineers also designed public lavatories. These lavatories were convenient, but not private. Users sat on rows of seats, side by side!

Family life

To the Romans, a family included servants as well as a husband, wife and their children. The servants not only worked in the house, but lived there, too. In rich families, servants had their own quarters within the villas.

▶ Families spent much of their time in the kitchen. Servants helped the women of the household to prepare the meals.

326

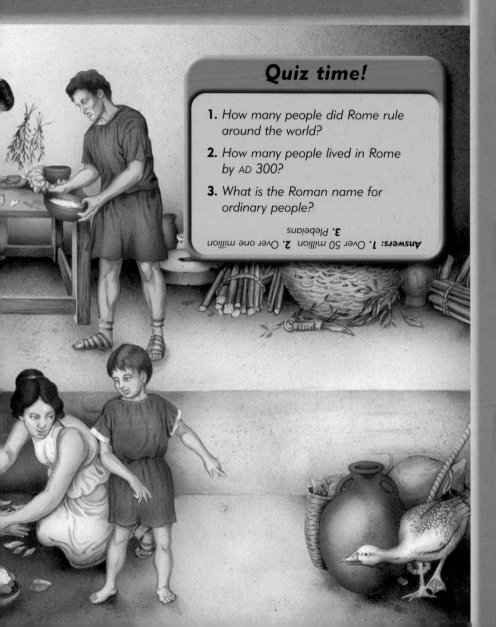

Quiz time!

1. How many people did Rome rule around the world?

2. How many people lived in Rome by AD 300?

3. What is the Roman name for ordinary people?

Answers: 1. Over 50 million 2. Over one million 3. Plebeians

Charcoal was burned in the stove.

Wine and oil were stored in large pots.

Herbs were ground up and put into sauces.

Eating and drinking

Most Romans ate very little during the day. They had bread and water for breakfast and a light snack of bread, cheese or fruit around midday. They ate their main meal at about 4 p.m. Rich people would have a meal with three courses. Poor people ate much simpler foods, such as lentil soup and barley porridge.

Make Roman pear mousse

You will need:
4 pears, peeled and cored • 6 eggs beaten
4 tablespoons of honey • oil • one teaspoon of cinnamon

1. Ask an adult for help. Mash the pears together with the honey, cinnamon and a splash of oil.

2. Add the beaten eggs and put the mixture into a oven-proof dish.

3. Cook in an oven for 30 minutes on a moderate heat. Let the mousse cool and then serve it to your family as a Roman treat!

Banquet food included roast meats, wine and dates.

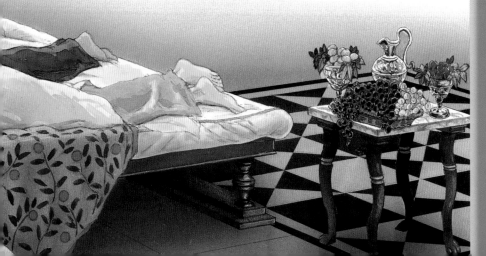

◀ At banquets, the Romans ate lying down on large couches arranged around a main table. They took off their sandals before entering the dining room.

Romans often wore crowns of flowers at banquets.

Silver jugs were used by rich people for serving wine.

329

A trip to the baths

Roman baths were more than just a place to get clean. They were also places to relax, meet friends and get fit. Visitors could take part in sports, do exercise, have a massage or a haircut. They could buy scented oils and perfumes, read a book or eat a snack. Or they could admire works of art in the baths' own gallery.

The frigidarium had the coldest pool

Fires heated the water for the hot rooms

Fun fact!

Although the Romans liked bathing, they only visited the baths once every fortnight!

The tepidarium had a cool or lukewarm pool

The hot room was called the caldarium

▲ There were public baths in most districts of Rome. Men and women were not allowed to bathe together. Women usually went to the baths in the mornings, while the men were at work. Men then went in the afternoons.

A massage was the perfect way to relax.

Baths were a good place to meet friends for a chat.

Washing was done without soap. Romans scraped the dirt off instead!

331

Roman style

Roman clothes were different depending on how important they were. Ordinary men and women wore plain white togas made of rough material. Rich people wore robes made of fine-quality wool and silk.

▲ At the height of the empire, women wore a brightly coloured robe and a shawl. Children wore knee-length tunics.

A Roman comb was made of ivory, bone or wood.

Wear a Roman toga

1. Drape a white sheet over your left shoulder. Now pass the rest behind your back.

2. Pull the sheet across your front, so that you're wrapped up in it.

3. Finally, drape the last end over your right hand and there you have it, a Roman toga!

Roman shoes had studs to stop them wearing down too quickly.

▶▼ Roman women wore fine jewellery made of gold and pearls. A shiny black stone called jet was carved into bangles and beads.

Necklace set with jewels

Gold earrings

Jet bangle

Gold ring

Hairstyles took a long time to fix and were kept in place with pins.

Learning new skills

Roman boys learnt three main subjects – reading, maths and public speaking. Boys needed all three skills for their future careers. There were no newspapers or television, so important people such as politicians had to make speeches in public. Boys went to school from 7 to 16 years old. Most girls did not go to school. They stayed at home where they learned how to look after the house.

▶ *Roman schoolboys were often taught by Greek schoolmasters because they were the best teachers. Learning to read and write were some of the most important skills.*

Let's speak Latin

puer	*POO-er*	boy	**mare**	*MAH-ray*	sea
puella	*poo-ELL-a*	girl	**insula**	*IN-soo-lah*	island
miles	*MEE-lays*	soldier	**equus**	*ec-WUSS*	horse

▶ Children used a counting frame called an abacus to help them to count.

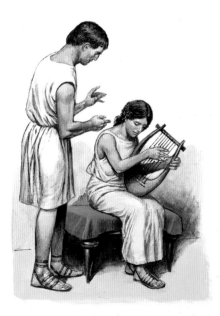

◀ Girls from rich families were taught to cook, clean and play instruments, such as the lyre.

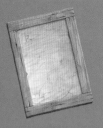

Wax tablets were used to write on.

Romans often read standing up as it was an easier way to read a papyrus scroll.

Ink was made of soot, vinegar and sticky gum. It was stored in a pot.

335

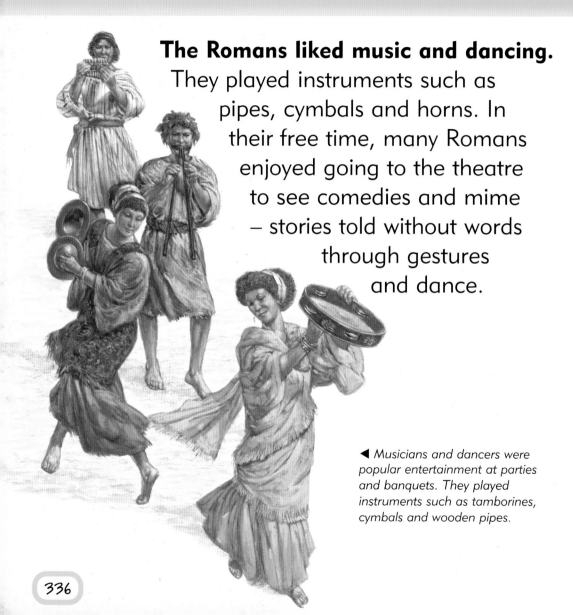

The Romans liked music and dancing.
They played instruments such as
pipes, cymbals and horns. In
their free time, many Romans
enjoyed going to the theatre
to see comedies and mime
– stories told without words
through gestures
and dance.

◄ *Musicians and dancers were
popular entertainment at parties
and banquets. They played
instruments such as tamborines,
cymbals and wooden pipes.*

Ancient Rome

▶ Women made their own clothes by spinning wool. There were no spinning wheels. Instead, the women twirled a spindle to stretch the wool into yarn. Then, the yarn was weaved into cloth.

Romans enjoyed acting in plays, but only men were allowed on stage.

Masks were often worn by actors to help identify the characters.

◀ Buskers played musical instruments in the streets, and they could even be hired for parties.

Fun fact!

Roman actors were so popular that women couldn't sit near the stage, in case they tried to arrange a date with one of the stars!

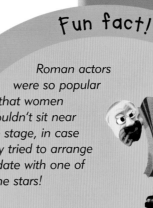

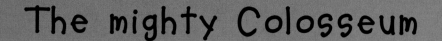

The mighty Colosseum

The Colosseum was a huge oval arena in the centre of Rome, which could seat 50,000 people. It was built of stone, concrete and marble and had 80 separate entrances. Outside it was decorated with statues of Roman heroes. This ampitheatre was used for gladiator fights and pretend sea battles.

6

5

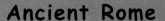

Colosseum key

① Awning (canvas roof)
② Tiered seating
③ Arena floor

④ Trapdoor
⑤ Underground tunnels
⑥ Stairs leading to seating areas

Gladiators had to fight in the arena until they died.

Gladiator helmets were decorated with plumes and crests to make them look more impressive.

Fun fact!

Gladiators became so popular that people wrote graffiti about them on the walls of buildings around Rome!

In the army

Being a soldier was a very good career, if you did not get killed! Roman soldiers were well paid and well cared for. The empire needed troops to defend its land against enemy attack. A soldier received good training in battle skills. When he retired after 20 or 25 years of service, he was given money or land to help him start a business.

▶ Soldiers used their shields to make a protective 'shell' called a testudo, or tortoise.

Fun fact!

Roman soldiers kept warm in cold countries by wearing woolly underpants beneath their tunics!

Ancient Rome

Quiz time!

1. Where did the Romans go to get clean?
2. What did ordinary men and women wear?
3. At what age did boys go to school?
4. What did children use to help them count?

Answers: 1. Baths **2.** Togas **3.** 7 to 16 years old **4.** Abacus

Roman cavalry rode horses and helped the foot soldiers during battle.

A Roman foot soldier had to carry a heavy pack.

A Gladius was a short sword with a very sharp point.

Roman roads

Rome's first main road was built in 312 BC.
All roads led to Rome. The city was at the
centre of a network of roads that stretched for
more than 85,000 kilometres. They had been
built to link every part of the empire to Rome,
so that Roman armies or government leaders
could travel more easily.

▶ *To make travel as quick as possible,
roads were built in straight lines, taking
the shortest route.*

Ancient Rome

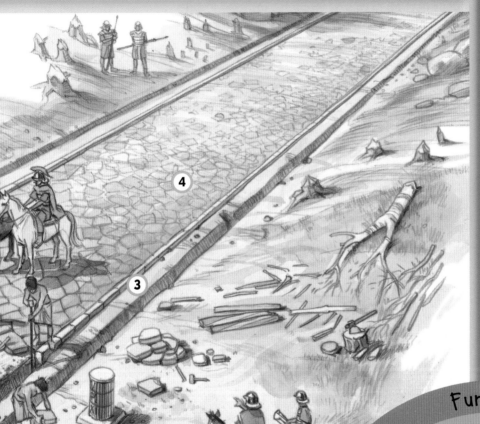

A road engineer used a 'grome' to measure straight lines.

Stone slabs were fitted together for a smooth road surface.

Key

① Route accurately marked out

② Solid foundations

③ Drainage ditch

④ Large surface slabs

Fun fact!

The Romans would often consult a priest or fortune-teller before setting out on a long journey.

Knights and Castles

During the Middle Ages, knights were soldiers
who rode on horseback and wore armour.
They served the king or the lord of a castle.
Read on to discover how castles were built,
which weapons knights used in battle and
what kind of food was eaten at a castle feast.

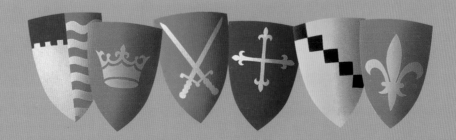

Life in the Middle Ages

In the Middle Ages, between 470 and 1450, many castles and forts were built. A castle provided shelter for a king or a lord and his family, and helped him to defend his lands.

▶ The castle was where soldiers were stationed, wrong-doers were imprisoned, courts settled disputes, weapons and armours were made, and great banquets were held.

Knights practising sword fighting

Castle capers

You will need:
pencil • paper • colouring pens

1. Draw a plan of your ideal castle, making sure it has plenty of defences. Will it have arrow slits? Will the walls be high? Will it have a moat running around it?

2. Don't forget to design a drawbridge to let the lord and his family in and out of their castle.

Jousting tournament

Soldiers practised their fighting skills in the castle grounds.

Knights were soldiers who fought on horseback.

Peasants farmed the land around the castle.

The first ca
But they wer
easily, so fro
began to bui
castle gave b
against attac
bad weather.

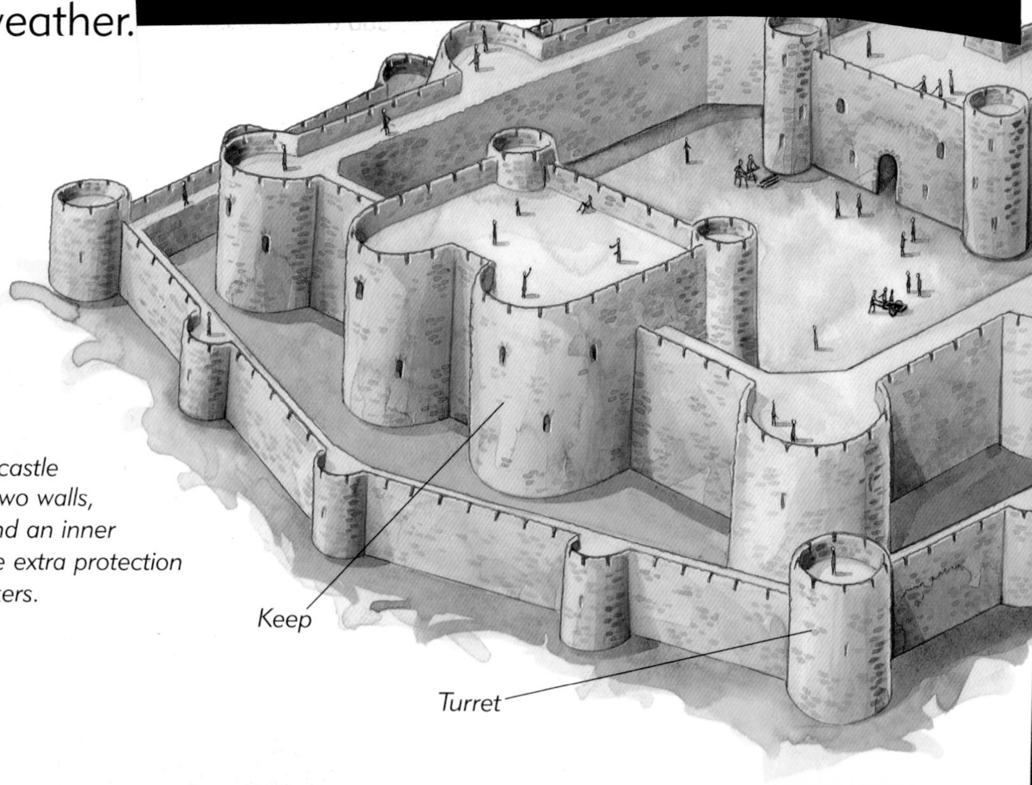

▶ A stone castle
often had two walls,
an outer and an inner
wall, to give extra protection
from attackers.

Keep

Turret

348

Knights and Castles

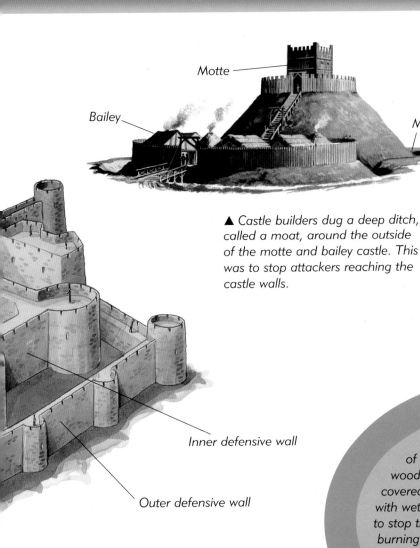

Motte

Bailey

Moat

▲ Castle builders dug a deep ditch, called a moat, around the outside of the motte and bailey castle. This was to stop attackers reaching the castle walls.

Inner defensive wall

Outer defensive wall

Archers stood on the castle walls and fired down at enemies.

Japanese castles were built with different layers.

Fun fact!

The builders of the early wooden castles covered the walls with wet leather – to stop them from burning down.

Building castles

The best place to build a castle was on top of a hill. A hilltop position gave good views over the surrounding countryside, making it harder for an enemy to launch a surprise attack.

Roughmason

Thick stone wall

Knights and Castles

Keep

Water wheel

Master mason

▼ Inside the castle was a big courtyard called a bailey. A thick wall was built around it. Most castles got water from a well that was dug inside the bailey. A large water wheel was used to draw the water up into the castle.

Workers who built the walls were called roughmasons.

The keep was the safest part of the castle, where the lord lived.

The master mason controlled the building of the castle.

Inside the castle

Stone castles were cold, damp places.
Cold winds blew through the
windows, which had no glass.
There was no heating
or running water.

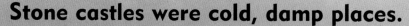

Knights and Castles

Castle key

1. Chapel tower
2. Prison tower
3. The Great Hall
4. Main gate
5. Kitchen
6. Garden
7. Dungeon
8. Bedroom

◄ The lord and lady did not live inside the castle alone. Servants and knights also had their own quarters. Even prisoners stayed in the castle – in the dungeon.

Kitchens were built far from the rest of the castle in case they caught fire.

Dungeons were dark, slimy prisons.

Tapestries were woven to hang on the castle walls.

Castle life

A castle was the home of an important and powerful person, such as a king, a lord or a knight. The lord controlled the castle itself, as well as the lands and people around it. The lady of the castle was in charge of the day-to-day running.

▼ Local villagers were allowed to shelter inside the castle walls when their lands were under attack.

◀ The master of the horse had to look after the lord's horses.

The steward was in charge of all the servants.

Servants cooked, cleaned and ran errands.

Armourer

Blacksmith

▲ The castle blacksmith made iron shoes for all the horses. The armourer made weapons and armour for the army.

Fun fact!

The servants didn't have their own bathroom. They had to take a dip in the local river to wash – and to get rid of any fleas and lice!

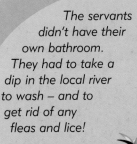

People and power

In the Middle Ages, the king or queen was the most important person in the country. The king gave land to his barons and other noblemen. In return, they supplied the king with soldiers and weapons to fight wars. This system of giving away land in return for services was known as feudalism.

Quiz time!

1. Who was in charge of the castle?

2. Where was the best place to build a castle?

3. Who made shoes for the horses?

4. Which room was built far away from the other rooms in case it caught fire?

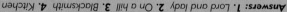
Answers: 1. Lord and lady 2. On a hill 3. Blacksmith 4. Kitchen

▶ In the Middle Ages, the Church and the ruler of the country were both very powerful, so they had to try to work together.

Barons were the most powerful of all noblemen.

Knights defended the king and lords from their enemies.

Peasants were the poorest people of the land.

Knight school

It took about 14 years of training to become a knight. At the age of seven, a boy was taught how to ride a horse and how to shoot a bow and arrow. He then became a squire, or assistant, where he learned how to fight with a sword. If he was good enough, he became a knight at the age of 21.

▶ The sons of noblemen were sent to a lord's house when they were seven years old. They spent 14 years with the lord, training to become knights.

Knights and Castles

▶ The ceremony of making a new knight was known as dubbing. A knight had to pray all night in church before his dubbing ceremony took place.

Swords with two sharp edges were used by knights in the Middle Ages.

A mace had deadly spikes to pierce armour.

◀ During the dubbing ceremony, a lord or another knight tapped the new knight on the shoulder with a sword.

Fun fact!

French knights wore shoes with pointed toes. When they needed to make a quick escape in battle, they had to cut the points off to run away!

Jousting tournaments

Knights often took part in pretend battles called tournaments. Tournaments were good practice for the real thing – war. Knights divided into two sides and fought each other as if in a proper battle.

Create your own shield

You will need:
coloured pens • paper

1. *Draw a big shield shape on a piece of paper.*

2. *On the shield, draw a symbol for your family – perhaps swords or a crown.*

3. *Colour in your shield, then hang it on your bedroom door to show everyone that you're a knight!*

Coats of arms were badges worn by knights so others could recognize them.

Banners displayed a knight's own personal design.

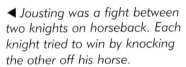
◀ *Jousting was a fight between two knights on horseback. Each knight tried to win by knocking the other off his horse.*

Fun fact!

Some knights cheated in jousts by wearing special armour that was fixed onto the horse's saddle!

Dress for battle

Early knights wore a type of armour called chainmail. It was made of thousands of tiny iron rings joined to each other. Gradually, knights began to wear more and more armour, until by the 1400s, they were wearing full suits of steel armour.

Knights and Castles

▼ Knights had two main weapons – the sword and the shield. They also fought with lances (long wooden spears), daggers and axes.

A wool tunic was worn over the top of a knight's armour.

Chainmail was a kind of 'knitted' metal armour.

Fun fact!

Soldiers called 'retrievers' had to run into the middle of the battle and collect all the spare arrows!

Brave knights

Many famous stories, or legends, have been written about knights and their bravery. The legend of St George tells how he killed a fierce dragon. King Arthur became king after pulling a magic sword, called Excalibur, out of a stone. Lancelot, Arthur's favourite knight, fell in love with Arthur's wife, Guinevere.

Quiz time!

1. What was the ceremony of making a new knight called?

2. What type of armour did early knights wear?

3. What were a knight's two main weapons in battle?

4. How long did it take to train a knight?

Answers: 1. Dubbing 2. Chainmail 3. Sword and shield 4. 14 years

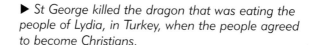

▶ St George killed the dragon that was eating the people of Lydia, in Turkey, when the people agreed to become Christians.

Knights and Castles

El Cid was a Spanish knight who fought against the Moors of North Africa.

The Black Prince was a great English warrior.

King Arthur had followers called the Knights of the Round Table.

Famous battles

Between 1337 and 1453, England and France were at war. This was called the Hundred Years War. The two countries fought each other to decide who should control France. In the end the French won, and England lost all of its lands in France except for the port of Calais.

▼ *In 1429, a young French girl called Joan of Arc led the French army to victory against the English.*

William the Conqueror claimed that he should be king of England.

▲ The Bayeux Tapestry is over 70 metres long. It records the story of the Norman invasion of England in 1066.

Knights used a weapon called the morning star – a spiked ball on the end of a chain.

Fun fact!

If a knight was captured alive during battle, he could be offered back to his family in return for a generous amount of money!

Fighting back

An attacking enemy had to break through a castle's defences to get inside its walls. Defenders would pull up the castle drawbridge and lower an iron gate, called a portcullis. Archers would fire arrows at the enemy through narrow slits in the thick castle walls.

Weapons key

① Large wooden shield
② Battering ram
③ Heavy stone
④ Crossbow
⑤ Boiling water

▶ Defenders of the castle used many different methods to try to keep their enemies out. They threw stone missiles, fired arrows and even poured boiling water over the castle walls.

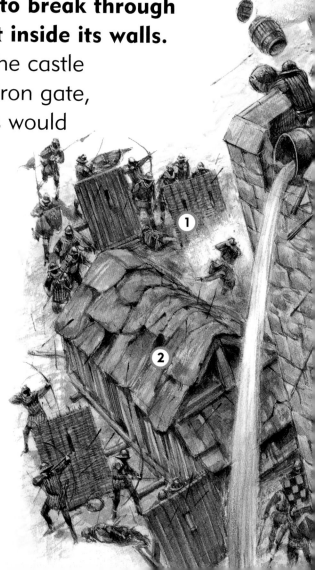

Knights and Castles

3

4

5

Boiling water was poured onto the heads of enemies.

A battering ram was used to try to break down the drawbridge.

Heavy stones were thrown onto the enemy below.

The crusades

The crusades were military expeditions from Europe to Palestine, in the Middle East.
Muslim Turks had seized control of Palestine. European Christians, known as the crusaders, set out to recapture Palestine from them.

Quiz time!

1. How long is the Bayeux Tapestry?

2. What were the followers of King Arthur called?

3. Who killed a fierce dragon in the famous legend?

Answers: 1. 70 metres
2. Knights of the Round Table 3. St George

370

Knights and Castles

▼ The crusaders built huge castles to defend their lands against the much larger Muslim armies. Although many soldiers were killed in the battles, there were four separate crusades between 1096 and 1204.

Saladin was a Muslim leader who fought against the crusaders.

Richard the Lionheart was an English king who led the Third Crusade.

Fun fact!

A crusader knight would share his tent with his beloved horse – it must have been a bit of a squeeze!

Castle siege

A siege is when an enemy surrounds a castle and stops all supplies from reaching the people inside. The idea is to starve them until they surrender or die.

Castle seige key

① Castle battlement
② Wooden shield
③ Giant catapult
④ Archer
⑤ Belfry

▶ Enemies attacked the castle using giant catapults to fire burning pieces of wood and stones inside the castle walls. The belfry was a tall tower where the attackers could fire directly at the defenders in the battlements.

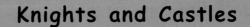

A crossbow was a more accurate weapon than a bow and arrow.

The trebuchet had a wooden arm with a sling to fire stones at the castle.

Fun fact!

The ropes used to wind up trebuchet machines were made from plaits of human hair!

Index

A

Abu Simbel 292
acid 23, 68, 121
acoustics 116
air 12, 84, 96, 122
    astronauts 38
    convection 113
    Moon 20, 48
    sound 116, 117
    weather 86, 88, 98
aircraft 12
albatrosses 186, 227
Alexander the Great 297
algae 67
Allosaurus 153
Anchisaurus 143
anemones 78, 81
anglerfish 177
Ankylosaurus 162, 163
ant lion 259
antbirds 240, 241
Antarctic 208, 236, 246, 247
antelopes 200
ants 205, 254, 255, 258, 268
Anubis 289
apes 212
Apatosaurus 151
Apollo missions 46, 47
aqueduct 318

arachnids 252, 257, 276, 280, 281
arches 318, 319
archers 349, 368, 372
Arctic 208, 209, 246, 247
Arctic terns 185
Argentinosaurus 151
armour 162, 362–363
army 296, 324, 340–341, 342, 366
armourer 355
Arthur, King 364, 365
artists 311
astronauts 12, 13, 20, 38–39, 40, 41, 46, 47, 48
astronomers 30, 34, 45
atmosphere 13, 18, 20, 53, 84–85, 86, 88
    planets 17, 24
atoms 118, 120, 132–133
Augustus 320
auroras 105
axles 130

B

badgers 204
bailey 349, 351
banquets 329
barnacles 173

barons 356, 357
Barosaurus 143, 150, 151
baths, Roman 330–331
bats 198, 202, 203, 212, 217
battles 366–367
battery 121
battlements 373
Bayeux Tapestry 367
bears 208, 219
beavers 193
bees 258
beetles 253, 263, 265, 266, 267, 268, 269, 271, 274, 275, 278
belfry 372
birds 135, 186, 187, 222–223
    anatomy 224
    babies 230, 231, 228, 229
    beaks 223, 240
    eggs 222, 228, 232, 233
    flight 234–235
    nests 232–233
    penguins 188, 189, 246
    rainforest 244–245
    river 248–249
    snow 246–247
    water 248–249
birds of paradise 244
birds of prey 227, 242–243

Black Prince 365
blacksmith 355
blubber 182
bluebottles 254
boars 219
boats 285, 308, 309
bones 224
breathing 13, 84, 85, 133, 172, 178, 228
Brachiosaurus 151
bricks 304, 305
bugs 275
buildings 108, 318–319
burrows 204, 214, 268
buskers 337
butterflies 202, 254, 260, 261, 272, 273

C

Caesar, Julius 321
camel 71, 95, 214
camera 39, 43, 115, 124, 125
camouflage 179, 188, 272–273
capybara 199
caracals 219
carbon dioxide 68
carbon fibre 130

carnivores 141, 145, 163, 218–219
cars 112, 130–131
castles 346, 347, 348–349, 352–353
  building 350–351
  defences 368–369
  life 354–355
  siege 372–373
caterpillars 273, 275
caves 68–69
CDs 126, 127
centipedes 257
ceramics 131
Cetiosaurus 143
chainmail 362, 363
chariots 297
Charon 24, 25
cheetahs 156, 200
chimpanzees 194
Christians 370
Church 356
cicadas 269
civets 212, 213
clams 81, 176
climate 73, 86, 87
clothing 307
clouds 44, 52, 89, 100, 101, 102
  planets 23, 26, 28, 29

clouds (*continued*)
  water cycle 96, 97
coats of arms 361
cochlea 117
cockroaches 264, 265
Coelophysis 157
cold-blooded animals 174–175
colonies, insects 258–259
Colosseum, Rome 338
colours 104, 114, 123, 126, 272
communication satellites 44
compass 35
composite materials 131
computers 108, 118, 124–125, 128, 129
condors 227
conduction 113
coniferous forest 72, 73
constellations 34–35
continental shelf 76, 77
continents 53
convection 113
coral reefs 77, 80–81
core, Earth's 54, 55
Corythosaurus 155
cosmonauts 40
crab spiders 279
crabs 78, 79

Index

craftworkers 302
craneflies 254, 268, 269
craters 21, 25, 49, 53, 67
Cretaceous Period 142
crickets 253, 263, 259
crocodiles 145, 149
crossbow 373
crusades 370–371
crust, Earth's 21, 49, 54, 55, 58, 64

D

damselflies 266
decibels 117
deep-sea creatures 176–177
deer 199
delta 66
deserts 70–71, 86, 94, 95, 214–215, 222, 280
devil's coach-horse 265
Diana 323
Dilophosaurus 143
Dimetrodon 144
dinosaurs 140–141, 146–147, 156–157, 168
  Age of 142–143, 150, 152
  defences 162–163
  end of 164–165
  evolution 144, 148

dinosaurs (continued)
  meat-eating 152–153
  plant-eating 141, 149, 162, 165
  senses 154–155
  young 158–159, 160–161
Diplodocus 151
dippers 248
discs 124, 125, 126, 127
doctors 312
dogs 218, 219
dolphins 172–173, 192, 194
  schools 210
dragonflies 260, 266
drawbridge 368
drought 95
drugs 136
dubbing ceremony 359
ducks 230, 231, 234, 235, 248
duck-billed platypus 196, 207
dunes 71
dungeons 353
dust storms 22, 95, 103
dusky titis 213

E

eagles 232, 242, 243
Earth 13, 17, 22, 48–49

Earth (continued)
  day and night 56–57
  eclipse 15, 57
  formation 52–53
  Moon 21, 46, 49
  orbit 90
  rocks 58
  satellites 45
  space 12, 13, 18–19
  structure 20–21, 22, 43, 54–55
eardrum 117
earthquakes 64–65
earwigs 254, 255, 268
ECG machine 136, 137
eclipse 15, 57
ecology 134, 135
eels 185
eggs
  birds 222, 228–229, 230, 231, 232, 233
  dinosaurs 158–159, 160
  insects 258
  mammals 196
Egyptian civilization 284
El Cid 365
electricity 120–121, 122
  Internet 128
  light 114
  magnets 119

electricity (*continued*)
  metal 130
  motors 118
  nerves 136
  television 123
  thunder 100
  wind 98
electromagnet 119
electrons 118, 120, 121, 123, 132, 133
elephants 156, 197, 198
email 128, 129
emperors 317, 320, 321, 322
energy 15, 31, 114, 120, 122
engines 36, 47, 112, 131
Eoraptor 141
Equator 34, 35, 86, 87, 92, 93
Erythosuchus 145
eucalyptus plants 195
Euoplocephalus 163
Eustreptospondylus 143
evaporation 97
evolution 144, 148–149
eyes 137, 154, 155, 239
Excalibur 364

F

falconet 227
falcons 230, 234

families 326–327
farming 300–301, 302, 347
fault line 65
feathers 189, 222, 223, 224, 225, 244
fennec foxes 215
ferns 149
feudalism 356
fibre 131
fins 178, 181
fireflies 261
fireworks 113
fish 78, 80, 81, 176, 177, 178–179
flamingo 223
fleas 262
flies 254, 256, 260
flight 202–203, 234–235, 260–261
flippers 182, 210, 236
flounder 179
flowers 274
food 303, 328–329
forces 16, 118
forests 72–73, 90, 212
forts 346
Forum, Rome 325
fossils 153, 154, 158, 159, 160, 164, 166–169, 168

front, weather 88, 89
fruitflies 254
fuel 36, 47
fulcrum 110
fur 182, 208, 214

G

galaxies 19, 32–33
gannets 187, 236, 237
gases 13, 18, 20, 36, 133
  space 14, 19, 28, 30, 31, 52, 53, 94
gears 111
geese 230, 234, 241, 248
generator 121
gerbil 214, 215
Giganotosaurus 153
gills 178, 267
giraffes 217
glaciers 75
gladiators 339
gliders 202
goddesses 288–289, 322–323
gods 288–289, 305, 322–323
grasshoppers 262
gravity 16, 30, 36
Great Bear 34, 35
great diving beetles 267
Great Hall at Karnak 293

Index

Great Pyramid 290–291
Great Red Spot 26, 27
grubs 268
guillemot 229
Guinevere 364

H

habitat 248
hadrosaurs 159
hailstones 101
hair 287, 307, 333
hares 199, 200, 201, 208, 209
Hatshepsut, Queen 287, 293
hawks 225, 230, 242
health 136
hearing 117
heart 136, 137, 224
heat 112–113, 130
hedgehogs 215
helium 133
herbivores 141, 143
herbs 327
herons 222, 248, 249
Herrerasaurus 141, 146, 147
hieroglyphics 310
hippopotamus 156, 206, 207
    hunting 308
honeybees 252, 271

hornbills 223, 233
hornets 271
horseflies 254
horsetails 149
Horus 289, 307
houseflies 255
houses 304–305, 326
hummingbirds 226, 227, 235
Hundred Years War 366–367
hunting dogs 219
hurricanes 99, 103
hydrogen 133

I

ice 17, 25, 27, 100
icebergs 45, 75
iguanas 174, 175
inclined plane 111
incubation 228, 231
insects 73, 252–253, 256, 264–265
    camouflage 272–273
    colonies 258–259
    mouthparts 270–271
    plant eaters 274–275
    soil 268–269
    water 266–267
International Space Station 40, 41

Internet 128–129
Io 27
iron 118, 119, 130
Isis 289
isobars 88

J

jacana 222, 249
jaguar 212
jewellery 333
Joan of Arc 366
jousting 347, 360–361
junglefowl 245
Juno 323
Jupiter (god) 323
Jupiter (planet) 17, 26–27
Jurassic Period 142, 143

K

kakapo 238
kangaroos 201
kangaroo rats 215
keep, castle 348, 351
keyboard 124, 125
Khafre 290
Khufu 291, 308
king crabs 281
kingfishers 222, 248

kings 320, 348, 354, 356–357
kitchens 353
kiwis 239
knights 346, 347, 357, 358–359
  armour 362–363
  castles 354, 355
  crusaders 370
  Hundred Years War 367
  jousting 360, 361
  legends 364–365
koalas 195

L

lacewings 271
ladybirds 254, 255
lakes 66–67, 68
Lancelot 364
land 13, 20, 48, 53
larvae 256, 259, 268, 269, 271, 275
laser light 126–127, 137
lava 60, 61
leafhoppers 263
leaf insects 272
leatherjackets 268
lemurs 202
lenses 115

leopards 73, 208
levers 110
light 104, 114–115
  deep-sea fish 177
  electricity 120
  fireflies 261
  Internet 128
  lasers 126–127
  mirage 95
  stars 14
light bulbs 108
lightning 100, 101
limestone 59, 68, 69
limpets 78
lions 195, 197, 218
lobsters 184
loudness 117
loudspeakers 118
Lunar Module 46, 47

M

macaws 244, 245
mace 359
machines 108, 110–111, 120, 122, 124, 136
maggots 256
magma 60, 61
magnetism 114, 118–119, 122, 135

Maiasaura 160, 161
make-up 306
mammals 192–193
  babies 195, 196–197
  desert 214–215
  digging 204–205
  families 194–195
  meat-eating 218–219
  plant-eating 216–217
  rainforests 212–213
  river 206–207
  running 200
  sea 182–183
  snow 208–209
  swimming 210–211
  whales and dolphins 172, 192, 194, 197, 210, 211
manatees 207
mantle 54
maps 44, 45, 88
Mars (god) 323
Mars (planet) 17, 22, 23, 42
marsh tits 241
masks 337
mason 350, 351
massage 331
Massospondylus 148
materials 130–131
mayflies 267

Index

meat eaters
  dinosaurs 141, 143, 145, 147, 149, 152–153, 162, 165
  mammals 218–219
  reptiles 145
  sharks 180
medicine 136–137
meerkats 195
Menkaure 290
merchants 298
Mercury (god) 323
Mercury (planet) 17, 18, 24–25
mergansers 235
Mesozoic Era 142
metals 54, 127, 130
meteorites 53, 85, 164, 165
meteorologists 88, 89
microchips 124, 125
microwaves 122, 128
Middle Ages 346–347, 356
migration 184–185
Milky Way 32, 33
millipedes 252, 256
minerals 67, 176
Minerva 323
mirage 95
mirrors 115
mites 257, 276

moat 349
moles 205, 269
monkeys 213, 217
monsoons 93
Moon 17, 19, 20, 21, 48, 49, 53
  eclipse 15, 57
  landings 46–47
moons 24, 25, 27
Moors 365
mosquitoes 261
moths 261
motte 349
mountains 12, 58, 62–63, 67, 97
mouse, computer 125
mouthparts, insect 270–271
mummification 294–295
muscles 136
music 116, 336–337
musk oxen 209
Muslim Turks 370, 371
Mussaurus 141
Muttaburrasaurus 157
myriapods 252

N

nature 134–135
nebula 19, 30–31

Neptune (god) 323
Neptune (planet) 16, 17, 28–29
Nero 321
nerves 136
nests
  birds 187, 189, 229, 232–233
  dinosaurs 158–159, 160, 161
  insects 258, 259
neutrons 132, 133
noise 116
North Pole 57, 87, 90, 91
nucleus 132, 133

O

oasis 71
oceans 18, 58, 74–75, 96
  deep sea 176–177
  seabed 76–77
Octavian 320, 321
oilbirds 239
okapi 213
opossums 197, 206
optics 114
orang-utans 193
orbit 57, 85, 90

Ornithomimus 147
Ornithosuchus 141, 145
Osiris 289
ospreys 249
ostriches 156, 223, 226
otters 183, 206, 207
owls 239, 240, 242, 247
oxygen 84, 85, 133, 178

P

palaeontologists 168
Pan 323
pandas 216
  red 193
pangolins 193
papyrus 285, 298, 307, 308,
  312, 313
Parasaurolophus 155
parents 222, 230–231
parrots 223, 225, 238, 245
peacocks 223
peafowl 245
peasants 347, 354, 357
pelicans 248, 249
penguins 188–189, 229, 230,
  231, 236, 237, 246
perching birds 224
pharaohs 286–287, 292,
  296

pigs 219
pigeons 225, 231
pinnipeds 182
planes 103, 112
planets 22–29
  Earth 20, 48, 52
  nebula 30, 31
  probes 42, 43
  Solar System 16, 17, 18
plankton 181
plant eaters
  dinosaurs 141, 149, 162,
    165
  insects 274–275
  mammals 216–217
plants 73, 134, 135, 145,
  148
plastics 112
Plateosaurus 149
platypus 196, 207
Plebeians 324
Pluto 16, 17, 24–25
poison 175, 270, 276, 279,
  281
polar bears 208
pollution 45, 134
pondskaters 267
poorwills 239
portcullis 368
pottos 212

power station 121, 134
praying mantis 270
pregnancy 197
prism 104, 114
Procompsognathus 141
pronghorn 200, 201
Protoceratops 158, 159,
  163
protons 132, 133
ptarmigan 247
puffins 187
pulleys 110, 111
pumas 197
pylons 121
pyramids 290–291

Q

queens 356
  termites 258
quetzal 245

R

rabbits 205, 217
radiation 38
radio 43, 116, 122, 123,
  128
radio beacons 135
radio tags 135

rain 68, 70, 72, 86, 89, 92, 93
  hurricanes 103
  rainbows 104–105
  rivers 66
  water cycle 96, 97
rainforests 72, 73, 92, 93
  birds 244–245
  mammals 202, 212–213
  scorpions 280
Ramses II 287, 292, 293
ravens 225, 243
reflection 115
reptiles 140, 144, 154, 158, 159, 174
Richard the Lionheart 371
Riojasaurus 149
River Nile 284–285, 308
rivers 66–67, 96, 97, 166, 248–249, 266
roads 342–343
roadrunners 235
robins 225
rock pools 78–79
rockets 36–37, 38
rodents 199
Roman Empire 316–317, 324–325
Rome 316
  building 318–319

Rome (*continued*)
  people 324–325
  roads 342–343
  rulers 320–321
  style 332–333
Romulus and Remus 320
Rutiodon 149

S

sailing 308–309
Saladin 371
Saltopus 141
sand 71
satellites 37, 44–45, 85, 122
Saturn 16, 17, 26–27
sauropods 150–151
Scaphonyx 141
Scelidosaurus 143
school 303, 334–335
science 108–109
scorpionflies 255
scorpions 276, 280–281
screws 110, 111
scribes 302
sea horses 81
sea lions 182, 210
sea mount 77
seabirds 186–187
seals 182, 183, 209, 210

seas 13, 18, 58, 64, 75, 97, 166
seasons 90–91, 92–93, 300
Senate 321
senators 325
senses 154, 181, 238
servants 326, 355
setts 204
sharks 134, 177, 180–181
shields 340, 363
shieldbugs 273
ships 296, 309
shrews 199
shrimps 78
silver 130
Shunosaurus 143
skeleton 180, 224
slaves 317, 324
sloth 213
sloth bears 205
slugs 278
snails 257
snakes 175
snow 86, 208, 209 246–247
snow bunting 247
snow leopards 208, 209
soil 134, 268–269
Solar System 16–17, 18, 26
soldiers 296, 297, 317, 340, 347, 356, 363

sound 116–117
South Pole 57, 87, 90, 119
space probes 42–43
space shuttle 12, 36, 41
space station 40–41
spacecraft 20, 37, 38, 40, 42, 48
spacesuits 12, 20, 38, 39, 48
sparrows 241
sparrowhawks 231
speed of light 114, 122
Sphinx 291
spiders 252, 276–279, 281
Spinosaurus 153, 163
spittlebugs 275
sponges 78, 79
springtails 263
squire 358
squirrels 202, 203, 205
St George 364
stalactites 69
stalagmites 69
starfish 78, 79
stars 19, 30–31, 34, 52
    Egyptians 312
    galaxies 32–33
    Sun 14, 94
steel 112, 118, 119
steward 355
stick insects 272

stings 270, 271, 280
stonefly nymphs 265
storms 44, 86, 99, 103
    Earth's formation 53
    Jupiter 26, 27
streams 66, 68, 69, 248, 266
Struthiomimus 157
summer 90, 91, 104, 209, 246
Sun 14–15, 17, 31
    day and night 56, 57
    Earth's formation 52
    god 288, 292
    Milky Way 32
    Moon 21, 49
    planets 16, 18, 22, 25
    seasons 90, 91
    tropics 93
    water cycle 96
    weather 94–95
swallows 235
swans 225, 231, 247
swifts 234
swiflets 233
swords 358, 359, 363, 364

T

tarantulas 279
Tarquin the Proud 320

tapestries 353, 367
tapirs 213
telephones 129
telescopes 45
television 116, 122, 123
temperate climate 86, 87
temperate forest 72, 73
temples 285, 292–293, 312
termites 205, 258, 259, 268, 275
theatre 336, 337
Thecodontosaurus 141
therapsids 145
thermometer 113
thorax 260, 261
thornbugs 273
thrush, song 222
thunder 89, 100–101, 102, 104
ticks 257, 276
tidal wave 165
tigers 218
togas 332, 333
tombs 291, 292–293, 310
tornadoes 102–103
toucans 241
tournaments 360
trade 298–299
transport 284, 308

Index

trebuchet 373
tree ferns 145
trees 72, 90
Triassic Period 142
Triceratops 163
Troodon 154, 155
tropical climate 86
tropics 92–93
Tuareg Arabs 94
tundra 246
turbines 98
turret 348
Tutankhamun 293
Tyrannosaurus 152, 153 162, 167

U

Universe 45
Uranus 16, 17, 28–29

V

Valley of the Kings 292
Velociraptor 166
venom 175
Venus (god) 323
Venus (planet) 17, 18, 22–23
vibrations 117
Viking spacecraft 42

volcanoes 59, 60–61, 63
  dinosaurs 165
  Earth 20, 48, 53, 55
  Io 27
  islands 76, 77
  Mars 23
Voyager probes 43
vultures 241

W

walruses 182, 183, 209
warm-blooded animals 172, 182, 192
wars 296–297, 356, 366–367
wasps 253, 259, 271
water 18, 20, 48, 71, 74
water boatmen 267
water birds 248–249
water cycle 96–97
water insects 266–267
water rats 206
water scorpions 267
water wheel 351
waves 122–123
  light 114, 115, 122, 126
  ocean 64, 75, 78
  sound 116, 117
weapons 296–297, 355, 356, 363, 367, 368, 373

weather 44, 72, 84, 86–89, 92, 98
weaver birds 233
whales 172–173, 185, 197, 198, 210, 211
wheels 110, 111
wigs 307
William the Conqueror 367
wind 22, 88, 89, 93, 98–99, 103
wings
  bats 202
  birds 222, 225, 227, 235, 243
  insects 260–261
  penguins 189, 236
winter 90, 91, 209
wolves 218
World Wide Web 129
worms 176
writing 302, 303, 310, 313
wrybills 223

X Y Z

X-rays 122
Yunnanosaurus 143
zebras 195